CW01082641

Ralph Allen
Builder of Bath

Diana Winsor

© Diana Winsor 2010

All rights reserved. No part of this publication may be reproduced or transmitted in any form or by any means, electronic or mechanical, including photocopying, recording, or any information storage and retrieval system, without prior permission in writing from the publisher. The right of Diana Winsor to be identified as the author of this work has been asserted by her in accordance with the Copyright, Designs and Patents Act 1988.

ISBN 978-0955954160

British Library Cataloging in Publication Data.
A catalogue record for this book is available from the British Library.

Published by
Polperro Heritage Press
Clifton-upon-Teme
Worcestershire WR6 6EN
United Kingdom
polperro.press@virgin.net

Printed by
Orphans Press Ltd
Leominster
Herefordshire
HR6 0LD
United Kingdom

Cover design by Steve Bowgen

ILLUSTRATIONS

Illustrations 3-17 by the author. Page decorations are those used by Bath's Georgian printers.
(courtesy of Georgian Imprints)

INTRODUCTION

Ralph Allen was not a writer. He left no copious correspondence. His definitive biographer, Benjamin Boyce, a Harvard professor who became interested in Allen in the 1960s, described his prose – appropriately - as 'direct, concise, and as barren as stone'. It is in looking at what he did, and how people reacted to his character, that we can get to know him.

He was essentially a businessman, often engrossed in exactly that – his business. Money must have meant a good deal to him, since his background was neither wealthy nor aristocratic. His reputation certainly mattered to him. But he loved books – when he first came to Bath one of his first ports of call was to a bookshop. His interests were wide and eclectic. He was a generous host and a compassionate friend, even when he felt he had to take a different view, as he did with William Pitt, for which he was the subject of much criticism.

The 18th century was one of just such innovation and entrepreneurial flair as Ralph Allen displayed. In taking the liberty of using the diary and letter form for his story, as did many writers of his time, I hope I have captured something of the man. Some of his letters were destroyed after his death, but where I have been able to use them, I have done so. The diary entries are imagined, although the events and context of his life are real. Where his own words or those of his contemporaries can be used, I have used them. Where I have included letters, or extracts of letters by others, they are authentic.

The illustrations are of people or places contemporary with Allen's own time.

His Christian name, incidentally, is normally pronounced with the 'l' included, and a short 'a', but it seems more likely that it was used with its alternative pronunciation, 'Rafe'.

THE DIARY OF RALPH ALLEN BUILDER OF BATH

Everybody knows Bath. Hot springs, the Romans, Georgian architecture and Bath Buns. 'A Queen enchanted' the poet Swinburne called it: 'England's Florence'. It is an architectural monument to humanity's weakness, hypochondria and frivolity, set in a bowl of hills under a soft Somerset sky.

At its heart is a spring of eternally hot water, whose powers of healing go back to ancient legend and the story of an exiled prince. Bladud, sent from court because of some disfiguring skin disease, became a swineherd. As his pigs wallowed in the steaming mud of the spring he saw that sores on their skin appeared to heal. Curious, he followed them into the muddy water, and found that the lesions on his own skin were clearing. He returned to court and in time became King Bladud. In about 500 BC the place of the hot springs was dedicated as a sacred shrine.

In the first century AD the Romans built a rest camp here for their weary soldiers. In this damp northern island they recreated the fleshpots of Rome for men who hungered for home and sun on stone. They called it *Aquae Sulis*: the waters of Sul. With some diplomacy they incorporated the local deity in their new urban centre. The Roman army depended a great deal on locally recruited auxiliaries and native provincial administrators.

After four hundred years of Roman rule, the end of empire saw the Saxons add little but awed observation to its crumbling remains:

> "The roofs are fallen...
>   Let them pour
>   Into a sea of stone
>   The hot streams".

Nevertheless by the tenth century the Saxons had built a great abbey at Bath. They called the city *Hat Batha*, or *Akemanceaster*, the town of the sick man. The monks took control of the hot springs, and people continued to come to be healed. Bath became a quiet west country town with a sideline in medicine – and quackery.

It was in the early eighteenth century that Bath was to be transformed. Three men could be said to be the builders of this new city. It was said that Beau Nash, the Master of Ceremonies, made it fashionable, and that John Wood, the architect, made it beautiful. But Ralph Allen made it possible. So who was Ralph Allen?

THE STONE

Timber, brick and stone are the chief building materials of Britain, and of these stone is the material of great architecture. Perhaps the finest is limestone, and in particular West Country limestone, quarried out of the great Jurassic beds of freestone laid down some 150 million years ago under warm and shifting seas. It is not old in geological time, for by this time birds and mammals were beginning to flourish on the earth. The oldest rocks are several thousand million years old. But it is old compared to human civilisation – that began only about 5000 years ago.

Bath stone is called oolitic limestone, because it contains ooliths, tiny shells at the heart of the individual grains of of sand in the stone, formed by lime sediments in the sea building up around them. It is known as freestone, because it may be cut in any direction.

It is part of a huge spine of limestone beds that stretch from France to Yorkshire – Caen stone from northern France built Canterbury, and Yorkshire stone built the Houses of Parliament. Underground it is the colour of warm honey, but once exposed to the air it becomes paler and greyer. We forget now that it is also absorbent: the soot from thousands of chimneys once turned Bath black and tan. Extensive cleaning over the past decades, and smokeless zones, have made the stone pale again, except for a forgotten building here and there.

In 1819 Peter Egan described a visit to the stone quarries, or mines, at Combe Down:

"The lofty arches, or pillars, remaining in a craggy state, left by the excavators to let in light to the subterraneous passages and caverns which extend for a considerable way under the earth, most interestingly claim the attention of the explorer. The Great Oolite is distributed in thick beds, and separated into vast blocks by vertical fissures, the sides of which are frequently embossed by the most delicate stalactites, and beautiful spars of diversified crystallisation".

So much stone was cut out of these subterranean quarries that great voids were created under the surface of the earth. In places the village of Combe Down was supported on land less than two metres thick. In 2007 work began on a major programme of infilling the stone mines with foamed concrete.

The Romans probably quarried stone at Bath and at Box, preferring the hard 'corngrit' stone for their new town, and no doubt it was locally used in later Saxon and mediaeval times. In 1697 the Wiltshire antiquary John Aubrey told a story about the discovery of Hazelbury Quarry near Box:

"It is the eminentest freestone quarry in the West of England, Malmesbury and all round the Country of it. The old men's story is that St Aldhelm, riding over there, threw down his glove, and bade them dig, and they should find great treasure, meaning the quarry".

St Adhelm was a seventh century Anglo-Saxon abbot, later bishop of Sherborne, and he built both his Abbey at

Malmesbury and the ancient Saxon church of St Lawrence at Bradford-on-Avon with stone from Hazelbury,

The present Bath Abbey, which replaces the earlier Roman temple and two great abbeys built by the Saxons and, later, the Normans, is built of stone from Box and Combe Down. It took some 200 years to complete, suffering under Henry VIII's depredations until Queen Elizabeth I, shocked by the state of it, started a fund for its restoration.

At the turn of the seventeenth century Bath was chiefly built of stone, but rubble, rather than the cut smooth ashlar of the city's facades today. Roofs were thatched or tiled and gables overhung narrow streets where water ran in open drains. The mediaeval wall still surrounded the city.

Attempts to market Bath stone, as against other limestones like its silvery rival from the Isle of Portland, met with derision in some quarters. It was compared to Cheshire cheese, 'liable to breed maggots that would soon devour it'. But Ralph Allen and the architect John Wood knew Bath stone was not only beautiful but durable. To prove their point they built Allen's great mansion at Prior Park, overlooking the city of Bath, and thus established Bath stone as one of the great architectural mediums.

THE CITY

After the Roman abandonment of Britain in the fifth century there were 500 years of internecine skirmishing between Celt and Saxon, Saxon and Norseman, Christian and pagan chieftain. Then, in AD 973, a man who had already reigned for 14 years was crowned Edgar, king of England in the great Saxon abbey at Bath. For centuries afterwards the people of the city celebrated the day of Edgar's coronation, so vivid was the memory of peace brought by this descendant of King Alfred the Great. Even today the coronation of English kings and queens is based upon that ceremony.

Less than a hundred years later, the Normans invaded. The old freehold system was replaced by feudalism. Although slaves were no longer bought and sold, all men now were serfs, belonging to their manorial lords – who did not even speak their language. Women were called chattels. The cattle, pigs and sheep of the Saxons became the beef, pork and mutton of the Norman table. Saxon landowners were dispossessed, Saxon buildings demolished.

At Bath, the ancient priory, by then Benedictine, was given by King William Rufus to one of his physicians, Bishop John de Villula, who proceeded to buy the entire town, complete with its hot springs. Under his enthusiastic patronage Bath gained a reputation both for scholarship and healing, although it was not until some years later that Geoffrey of Monmouth wrote down the story of Prince Bladud and the pigs.

Bishop John also began the building of a vast new Norman cathedral to replace the old abbey, although he never saw it completed. A new priory was built and more land taken over by the monks, probably including the deep valley above Widcombe, where lakes bred carp for the refectory table. In its quiet cloisters may have studied the young Henry Plantagenet, who as Henry II was to temper Norman rule with his introduction of such enduring English principles as those of common law, the jury system and local government.

It was in Henry II's reign that Bishop Reginald Fitzjocelin founded the Hospital of St John in Bath, which dates from 1180. Bishop Reginald was chosen to attend Richard I at his coronation, and in 1189 Richard the Lionheart granted the city a charter giving it the right to run markets and fairs. The main street, Cheap Street - meaning Market Street - was then only seven feet wide with an open sewer down the middle, and all kinds of rubbish was thrown into the old Bum Ditch that ran across the watermeadows to the river. Now the city authorities began to clean things up a little.

The baths themselves were run by the monks purely for treating the sick, as the Benedictine order forbade bathing. By the time the sixteenth century writer John Leland described the baths, they were probably much as they had been for centuries. There were three: the Cross Bath, the Hot Bath, and the King's Bath. The Cross Bath was the largest:

"This Bath is much frequentid of people diseasid with Lepre, Pokkes, Scabbes and great Aches...The colour of the water is as were a depe blew sea water, and reeketh like a seething Pot continually, having sumwhat a sulpurous and sumwhat a pleasant flavour".

The monks were very powerful. Almost all the land around Bath was owned either by the priory in the city, or by other religious houses in the region. Trade made them rich, and the cloth trade was one of the most lucrative. Chaucer's Wife of Bath, who probably lived at Twerton, was a weaver 'very skilful in cloth making'. Daniel Defoe wrote that "many of the great families who now pass for gentry in the western counties have been originally raised from and built up this truly noble manufacture of cloth". Even when the Black Death scourged England in the fourteenth century, the monasteries grew fat. When the Bishop of Bath and Wells, Oliver King, visited Bath in 1499, he found the monks dissolute and their priory church half in ruins. Bishop King was responsible for planning the new abbey church which is essentially the one we see today – to the left of the west door you can see angels on a stone ladder, said to commemorate the dream which inspired him to build his abbey.

At the beginning of Queen Elizabeth I's reign people came to Bath for both for drinking the waters and bathing in them. They would drink ladlefuls of the hot water in the morning, before the bathers arrived, in the hope that it was then relatively clean... It was Queen Elizabeth who granted the city its second royal charter and handed all powers to the corporation rather than the clergy. She was roundly critical of the sewerage arrangements, and it wasn't until James I's queen, Anne of Denmark, came to find a cure for her dropsy in 1616 that the baths became a little more respectable, and visitors increased. Nevertheless in 1631 a certain Dr Jordan was pretty dismissive of the city:

> "The streets are dunghills, slaughterhouses and pigstyes. The butchers dress the meat at their own doors, while pigs wallow in the mire. The baths are

bear-gardens, where both sexes bathe promiscuously." He could not recommend the waters for internal use, as they could not be 'procured clear enough for drinking'.

Conscious of these shortcomings, Bath Corporation issued a set of byelaws in 1646. Typical of them was:

"...no person shall presume to cast or throw any dog, bitch or other live beast into any of the said Baths, under the penalty of three shillings and fourpence. That no person shall thrust, cast, or throw another into any of the said Baths with his or her clothes on, under a penalty of six shillings and eightpence..."

Things were improving, however. In 1668 Samuel Pepys visited – for his health – and although he commented that 'it cannot be clean to go so many bodies together in the same water', he quite enjoyed the experience. Celia Fiennes, one of those indefatigable lady travellers, came to Bath in 1695 and described the bathing. She wore a stiff canvas gown, stained yellow by the waters, and afterwards she changed into a flannel nightgown and was carried back to her lodgings in a sedan chair, to be put to bed 'to sweat'. She said the water tasted like the water 'that boils eggs'.

At the end of the seventeenth century Bath hadn't grown much since Roman times, and its abbey, plainer and stubbier then without its nineteenth century embellishments, shouldered its way out of a crowded nest of half-timbered houses, beaten earth alleyways, piggeries and gardens. At the East Gate on the river watermills turned, and there was a bustling fish market. Beyond the city's mediaeval walls were the open meadows of King's Mead, the Ambry and the Ham. In winter a miasma of coal and woodsmoke hung over the town and in summer there was a pervading smell of refuse and dungheaps.

Yet the little city was prospering on its reputation as a reasonable small country resort with very efficacious hot springs. It was attracting a lot of liverish people who could afford the fees of a growing multitude of doctors, and it was getting cleaner. The Corporation even built public lavatories, 'Houses of Ease'. London was thin of company in summer, and God knew the country was dull enough. Oliver Goldsmith observed: 'They wanted some place where they might have each other's company, and win each other's money, as they had done during the winter in town'.

They tried Bath. It was small and a trifle tawdry, with nowhere to dance but the Town Hall, with a lot of country bumpkins – people of rank did not mix with hoi polloi if they could avoid it – but the baths were diverting and the gaming was good. Queen Anne decided to visit in 1702 and again in 1703, and all at once Bath was *the* place to go. Defoe remarked sourly: 'We may say now it is the resort of the sound as well as the sick and a place that helps the indolent and the gay to commit that worst of murders – to kill time'.

By the beginning of the eighteenth century Bath had a population of less than 3,000 people. It was about to increase tenfold.

THE POSTMASTER

Ralph Allen was born on July 24, 1693, in the old North Cornish town of St Columb Major, where his baptism is recorded in the parish church. He was one of at least four children born to Philip Allen and his wife. There are no documented records of his father's occupation, but the family was respectable, and his grandparents, Reskymer and Gertrude Allen, seem to have run a shop, perhaps an inn. Local post offices were often run in conjunction with an inn, and there is a suggestion that Reskymer's widow Gertrude ran the post office business at St Columb for some years. That would mean the young Ralph probably helped his grandmother in the post office. He must have been a bright and eager boy with a good grasp of figures. He was only about 15 when he got a job in the post office at Exeter, where the Deputy Postmaster was one Joseph Quash. He did much to introduce new regulation into the workings of the postal system, but lost control of his own finances and went bankrupt in 1713.

Two years after joining Mr Quash at Exeter, Ralph Allen left and moved to the post office in Bath. He became Deputy Postmaster there at the age of 19. He went on to reform the postal system in England, winning a government contract which was regularly renewed over subsequent decades. At the same time he bought up all the stone quarries on the downs above Bath, and together with the architect John Wood established the reputation of the pale stone that had hitherto been disregarded as a material for fine architecture. He created a famous railway to carry the massive blocks of stone from the quarries down to a wharf on the River Avon, and invested in the successful project to make the river navigable to Bristol – and thence to London. He built houses for his workforce and planted more than 50,000 trees to ameliorate the effects of the quarrying on the downs

Yet although Ralph Allen was an acute businessman, an entrepreneur long before the word was current, he also loved books, family, friends – and beauty in landscape and architecture. His house at Prior Park was not only a manifestation of the glories of Bath stone, but a place where those who shared his enthusiasms – passion is perhaps too strong a word for this quiet, careful man – could enjoy good company and hospitality. He cared for the vulnerable both publicly and privately, never forgetting his humble Cornish boyhood. The Bath of gamblers and fashionable soirees was not for him, although he was a councillor and served as Mayor of the City. He preferred tranquil evenings with a book or good conversation, and enjoyed walking and riding his beloved horses in the countryside around his home.

Ralph Allen remained in Bath, with some summer excursions to Weymouth, to which he gave a certain social cachet, until he died at the age of 71 in 1764. His quarries were sold off and after several years Prior Park, its contents auctioned, was let. Few people outside his home of Combe Down know very much about him, although his name remains on the road where once thousands came to marvel at his ingenious railway.

DIARY
June 16 1710

Up at 3 o'clock three days past, and at 4 got into the Bath Coach, and set off. The Coach carried only 4 inside passengers. I would rather have ridden for the roads are very bad except on the approach to Bath, where the road has been turn-piked. However I was much encumbered with goods and some books which weigh heavy. We had a very fat woman with a dog and many band boxes in the coach, which much incommoded us. We breakfasted at Taunton on coffee and tea, for which I paid 2 shillings. We were very near meeting with an accident, passing a wagon, but thank God we got by safe and well.

Arrived in darkness, but arrangements had been made for me to put up at The Black Swan in Broad Street, where I supped and slept well, tho v noisy with wagons passing from the nearby Wiltshire's yard. Breakfasted there this morning, a very genteel breakfast indeed, coffee and tea, bread and butter, cold tongue etc. Afterwards I walked to the Abbey and took a turn around the city before meeting Mrs Collins, the deputy here. The place lies low in a bottom with steep ascents all ways out of the town, encompassed by high hills and woods. There are some new lodging houses, tho many indifferent, but the streets are of a good size and well pitched.

The Abbey is lofty and spacious, and a pleasant green beside it. I also came upon another pleasant place for diversion, the King's Mead, a green meadow for walking, with several little cake-houses where you can have fruit syllabubs and summer liqueurs to entertain the company. There are no coaches there - indeed there is little use of a coach only to bring people to the city, for the ways are not proper for coaches, all is adapted to the bathing and drinking of the waters, so the streets are clean kept and there are chairs as in London to carry the better sort of people in visits, or if sick and infirm.

The air must be affected by the Baths, of which there are five close to the Abbey church: the small Hot bath, then another called the Lepers, the third being the Cross bath with seats round it for the gentlemen to sit and arches with seats for the ladies – all stone, but they will give you a cushion. I believe this bath to be the most fashionable. The King's Bath is very large, and the hot springs bubble up so fast and so strong they must be hot against the bottoms of one's feet. Ladies go into the bath with garments made of a fine yellow canvas, which is stiff and made large with great sleeves like a parson's gown, and the gentlemen have drawers and waistcoats of the same sort of canvas. Afterwards they are wrapped in flannel nightgowns. All the baths are open to the sky, so in cold weather there must be much steaming and wetness – this morning the sky was, luckily, blue.

The Queen's Bath is not so big. I had a taste of the water from the pump in a gallery of the King's Bath, and indeed it tastes like the water that boils eggs. When the baths are empty, sometime after

11 of the clock in the morning, there is a white scum on the water which is skimmed off before any company goes in. I have no great desire myself to try this water, since I have no ailment requiring cure, but I have observed the many Chairs that pass by in the street, carrying the bathers to their lodgings wherein I understand they lie and sweat it out. For myself, I prefer the new bath near The White Hart in Widcombe, across the river, for it is cold, and I might venture, the healthier for it.

There is no doubt that the two visits of the Queen have done much to improve the place: St John's Hospital, the almshouse close by the Cross Bath, is being restored, and there is a new row of houses along the gravel walks east of the Abbey which I declare are very handsome. The thatch of many of the roofs is being replaced with tile, and casement windows with sashes. Householders are supposed to burn candles or lamps outside their properties in the winter months, to make the streets safer. There are orchards and gardens leading down to the river Avon, and I am told the markets are very good here with much provision of flesh and fish. There is a master of ceremonies in the Pump Room and Harrison's Rooms, Master Richard Nash – he is known as 'Beau' – who has brought some decorum to the crowds here. And there are indeed crowds, with many entertainments, chocolate houses, bowling, puppet shows and plays. I have made brief acquaintance with Mr Nash, who is perhaps twenty years my senior, red-faced with an air of command about him, though I venture to suggest not all take him entirely seriously. He wears a black wig and cream coloured hat so he does not go unnoticed. Nevertheless he has influence, and I must needs improve such acquaintance if I am to progress in this city.

Letter from Ralph Allen to Gertrude Allen
November 7 1710

My Dear Grandmother,
I have now been in post this six months, and have found the work both exacting and absorbing. Mrs Collins is a hard-working woman and her husband has an alehouse in Westgate Street, adjacent to the post office which is still in a part of the old church of St Michael's, near to the Cross Bath. On one of the windows various lines have been written, including these:

> *Bath for distinction may cope with old Rome,*
> *But sulphur and fire are reserved for both's doom.*

And:

> *Oh ye gods, what have I done?*
> *Spent all my money and had no fun*

I have a room here which is small but clean. There is little space in any case: the two businesses, alehouse and post office, find themselves occupying the same premises, according to trade, as indeed happens in Cornwall as elsewhere. Mrs Collins receives £25 annually as her salary from the Postmaster General in London, and it would be sorely insufficient to support her were it not for the tavern. I have been to some extent employed in both, which has given me some more income.

You of course understand this business, and know how much depends upon the honesty of the Deputy Postmaster. Each month he (or she) must report to the Postmaster General in London the amount of postage taken in by him (or quarterly, as in your own case), and subsequently remit that sum. But there is so much opportunity for vagueness, or outright dishonesty, through the pocketing of fees from travellers riding post, or through the Deputy being able to send and receive his own letters free, or indeed extracting gratuities for local deliveries, that I am sure the system could be improved. The rules are full of gaps and ambiguities.

In particular I have been studying the working of the bye-way and cross post letters. As you know, those letters that pass along one of the six main roads out of London but neither start nor stop in London are called bye-way letters: the cross-post letters now pass between cities and towns without having to go through London at all. Of course it was Mr Quash at Exeter who made me see how the thing may work. If everyone did his duty along the route there would be a precise record of all these bye-way letters, the prepayments all being collected and noted by each postmaster on the route. The service could be reliable and prompt. There are some 300 such postmasters in England and if this system was properly observed, they would make sufficient rewards, and the Postmaster General would collect a large income for the Treasury. I do not think Mr Quash was quite aware of the importance of adhering strictly to the system

As it is, there are not sufficient post offices, and people often send letters by carters or coaches. And there are evident inequities in the particular layout of the roads. Two towns quite close together might be served by different main post roads, of which of course there are still only six, all from London, and mail between them might therefore travel along one road to London and be sent out from there on another. The dissemination of printed directions and warnings to all the post offices merely teaches men to be dishonest, and the dishonest to be more cautious. I believe that every postmaster should check, and be checked by, every other. It is my view that if you dismiss a rogue you will be sure to get a greater one in his stead, and that you must therefore seek to make the rogue see that honesty will, in the long run, pay him better.

When, indeed, I have stumbled upon some such irregularity or violation of the rules, I have endeavoured simply to smile upon the wrongdoer and make it clear to him that no false pretence or evasion can deceive me. Few can resist such an appeal to his sense of right, and fail to conform to the principle of duty.

I do not think it would be so difficult to make improvements. Yet perhaps it is because the Lords of the Treasury, who control it, do not see the Post Office as a service to the nation, but as a source of revenue, that no such improvements have yet been made. I believe I can make it my business to demonstrate that improvement may be rewarding to both the Government and the general populace.

Your loving Grandson,
Ralph

DIARY
1712 March 26

I was today appointed Deputy Postmaster of the Bath Post Office, in place of Mrs Collins, although for a time I shall continue to assist her in the inn, as my salary will also be no more than £25 per annum. However I am now in a position to make progress. My first duties will be to further my acquisition of the cross-road posts at present covered by the Mr Joseph Quash in Exeter, whose territory covers all the important towns in Somerset, Devon, Gloucestershire, Worcestershire, Herefordshire, Oxfordshire, Shropshire and South Wales. I learned much from Mr Quash, but I fear his application and his competency with the financial aspects of the business have led him into some difficulty.

Letter from Ralph Allen to Gertrude Allen
February 18 1713

My Dear Grandparents,
You will no doubt have heard of the prosecution
of Mr Quash and the deprivation of his postal
authority in Exeter. I must admit to sadness
for Mr Quash for I know to him to be a man of
energy and imagination, only his understanding
of the practicalities of the business being deficient
and thereby causing his downfall. However I
am the beneficiary of his failure. I have been in
communication with a number of other postmasters
in the territory, and we have taken over all Mr
Quash's cross-posts. I believe my salary from
the Postmaster General will be augmented by
approximately £130 a year, which for a man not
yet twenty gives me – and I hope you – some
satisfaction. It is, I would hazard, a better route
than that affording here in Bath by the gaming
rooms presided over by Beau Nash. And I assure
you this will not the end of my plans.

The weather has been very wet and icy of late and
I saw a man on a fine grey horse slip and take a
bad tumble on the road up to Lansdowne Hill out
of the City.

I am becoming much acquainted with people here
in Bath, and spend a good deal of such free time as
I have in some of the excellent bookshops. I have
just purchased a copy of Mr John Norris's Essay
'Towards the Theory of the Ideal or Intelligible
World', having already in my possession his

excellent 'A Practical Treatise concerning Humility', and have spent a pleasant hour or two entering in the margins all the corrections in the Errata list. I have attended church at St James's and made some acquaintance at the Pump Room, tho' it is not to my taste to be with so many jostling all together, and from the highest quality to the lowest-born, all directed by Mr Nash in a way which I marvel at so many being happy to comply. As to gambling – well, I am with Mr Defoe upon that matter: "The luxury of the age will be the ruin of the nation if not prevented. We leave trade to gain in stocks; we live above ourselves and barter our ready money for trifles."

Your aspiring Grandson,
Ralph

Queen Anne died in August 1714 and her German cousin was proclaimed George I of England. Many people would have preferred her half brother, James, although he was a Roman Catholic. Jacobite resentment began to be seen on the streets. There were riots in Bristol in October.

Letter from Ralph Allen to Philip Allen
August 25 1714

My Dear Father,
There is much talk of disaffection here in Bath following the passing of our Queen, and the proclamation of her German cousin as King George II of England. Her half brother might be a Papist but then he is, after all, English... Is there such unrest in Cornwall? I would suspect so, for it was always a place where a sense of independence lies in the very granite. Nevertheless I can have no such sentiments, for my loyalty to the Crown – to the Office, perhaps, rather than the man – must remain resolute. But you may inform me, perhaps, of any such talk.
Your loving son,
Ralph

Letter from Philip Allen to Ralph Allen
September 9 1714

Our Dear Ralph,
I write this with some hesitation, for I am one of those who possess the sense of independence to which you referred in your last letter. However it is true that there is some feeling against the new King here in Cornwall. It is no more than murmurings at present, but perhaps it is as well that you should be aware of it, for I would not want your connections here to have some unlooked for effect upon your position.
Yours affectionately,
Father

The following summer, public resentment began to boil over.

Letter from Ralph Allen to Philip Allen
August 4 1715

My Dear Father
In your last letter you made mention of certain new developments on the issue of disaffection in the area. I would ask that you inform me of what intelligence you may have in order that I can take action accordingly. The Jacobites have a strong hold here in Bath and I understand that at least one regiment of horse will be ordered to march upon those whose Stuart sympathies have led them into some foolhardiness in this matter, namely some conspiracies against His Majesty. Any such intelligence will of course be communicated to no one save those directly concerned.
Your dear Ralph

Letter from Philip Allen to Ralph Allen
September 16 1715

Our Dear Ralph,
I enclose herewith knowledge of which you may be unaware, tho' tis common I believe that in this part of Cornwall, and indeed others, there are many common people ripe for rebellion. Here in St Columb some six or seven people publicly proclaimed the Pretender, and two have been arrested, with a reward of £100 offered by the Government for the capture of the others. I have

to tell you that they were not alone, and they and others have been gathering together arms and horses for the purposes of moving north towards Bristol: namely, some two hundred horses, chests of firearms, cannon, swords, and indeed a mortar and moulds to cast cannon. I have no direct evidence for this, but you may take my words that is known by many more than have so far attracted serious attention here.

Your loyal Father

Letter from Ralph Allen to Major-General George Wade

October 9 1715

Sir

Having read in the London Post-Man that you have been ordered to Bath to suppress the designs of disaffected people in this area, I would crave a meeting at the soonest opportunity in order to divulge some information which I feel should be known to you. It is a most urgent matter concerning a shipment of arms from the West, that is, a wagon-load of firearms and other weaponry, together with horse transport. You will be aware that as Deputy Postmaster here and also myself a Cornishman, I am not to be doubted in this matter.

Your humble and obedient servant
Ralph Allen, Deputy Postmaster

And indeed he did attend on the Major-General, who subsequently seized the considerable quantity of horses, arms and cannon sent from 'the West'. At the end of October the anniversary of King George I's coronation was formally celebrated, despite any previous Jacobite sympathies in the town, with bell ringing, processions and fireworks. The only sour note occurred when a certain Josiah Priest was dismissed by the City Council as organist of the Abbey Church, because he was said to have spoken disrespectfully of the King. He was cleared of the accusation.

General Wade was 42, an Irishman who worked his way up through the army. He had fought in several foreign campaigns and accumulated a good deal of money along the way – and although a bachelor, he had by then four children, all of whom he cheerfully acknowledged and to whom he left major bequests in his will. He was a generous man with a keen eye for art and design and he liked the young Ralph Allen. Their friendship developed, and Wade built a house in Bath in 1720. Its elegant façade still survives on the Abbey Churchyard, as does Wade's Alley, a paved area which he had opened up along the north side of the Church to encourage people to walk outside from the baths to the promenades instead of – as they had done before – through the Abbey. He was elected as MP for Bath in 1722. He is famous for building some 250 miles of road and 40 bridges as part of the suppression of the Jacobite Rebellion in Scotland between 1725 and 1737.

For Ralph Allen it was another useful friendship to cultivate in pursuit of his immediate end – a Post Office contract to improve the postal system.

DIARY
April 14 1720

Well, 'tis done. On Friday last the contract was signed. It will extend for seven years, agreed by the Postmasters General Lord Cornwallis and Mr James Craggs. They granted my proposal partly – so it was said – because one of the surveyors sent out by them had examined my accounts strictly, and found that from the moment I entered my office I had faithfully reported all my bye-way letters - that is, that I had not, as so often indeed occurs, thrown all the bye-way letters that travel between two towns on one road and do not reach London, all into one sack. Also they were thus confident that I was energetic in combating the practice of demanding and receiving the Postage of all the bye-way letters before they were put into any of the country post offices, hence (from the general temptation of destroying these letters for the sake of the Postage) the joint mischiefs of embezzeling the Revenue and interrupting and obstructing the Commerce fell naturally in to support and inflame one another.

So be it. I now have a great task ahead of me, for I now control virtually all the English cross-road posts, the carriage and delivery of all bye-letters not going or coming from, to or through London, such mail services to be at least three times a week and at a speed of five miles an hour. I have charge of funds to pay all the deputy postmasters – and must have post horses available everywhere on a half-hour's notice.

The greatest work will be in compelling all the deputies (the postmasters) to do their work more correctly, more honestly and assiduously. I intend to set out within the month, with my servant Henry Lance, to make a survey of all the Kingdom. I shall study all the roads, the distances, the key towns and cross-roads. Wherever I find frauds I shall trace them fully and minutely through all their windings. It is true that I must pay an annual fee of £6,000 to the Government, but the surplus will be mine, and although it will take time I know that I have the unflagging energy and courage to see a profit in the end.

Which he did, and his contract, over the succeeding years, was always renewed with very little question until the death of King George II in 1760.

Letter from Ralph Allen to Miss Elizabeth Buckeridge
November 28 1720

Dear Miss Buckeridge,
The weather being not so clement that it is easy to make the trip into Hertfordshire, I would therefore wish to write in order to say what pleasure it gave me to make your acquaintance when I visited your brother and Mr and Mrs Hudson. Should there be opportunity for me to survey certain of the postmasters in the London area, I hope you would be at home and afford me such a welcome as I am bold enough to expect. Work keeps me very busy here, tho on Sunday I had the pleasure of visiting Mr John Hobbs at Bristol, to talk about the opening of the river passage between Bath and the seaport at Bristol.

Even following the Act of 1712, more than eight years ago, there has been little progress on opening up the navigable river passage on the Avon between Bath and Bristol, so much opposition is there to the very idea of it. However I believe it to be inevitable, as does Mr Hobbs, so we have great hope that we shall succeed with the project.

He pressed me to dine, but there being no moon and likewise some rain falling, I thought it prudent to return home, tho he loaned me an umbrella for the journey in his coach. The barometer is very low down but the weather will not prevent me travelling, if so encouraged, to see you again.
Your humble servant, Ralph

Letter from Ralph Allen to Gertrude Allen
January 13 1721

My Dear Grandmother,
You will know that I have had cause to visit London recently, and have taken the opportunity to visit the home of Mr and Mrs Anthony Buckeridge in Ware, Hertfordshire. Also there was Mr Buckeridge's sister Elizabeth, the younger of two of the late Seaborne Buckeridge, a London merchant who left her one-sixth of his estate. The elder sister, Sarah, is married to Mr Kendall Hudson. The family is prosperous – Mr Buckeridge owns a farm in Herefordshire and property in Fleet Street as well as his house, and others, in Ware, and his wife too has expectations from her aunt, wife of Sir Richard Tufton of Ware. Well, Elizabeth has consented to be my wife. I am very sensible of the advantage to me, as she is so well-connected and indeed so financially secure, but she accepted my proposal without hesitation (in the library at Mr Buckeridge's house, for we share a love of books, and were comparing one with another beside the fire when it came upon me to seize the moment). Already I believe I am myself accepted as a part of the family, and I am sure that you and Father and Mother will likewise find some mutual gratification in our union. The date is to be set for August, the 26th, at the Charterhouse Chapel in London, for she is formally of St Bride's Parish.

PS She is quite beautiful.
Ever your loving Grandson,
Ralph

Ralph Allen made a good marriage. Elizabeth Buckeridge's brother Anthony owned a considerable amount of land and property, and his wife Ann was wealthy in her own right. Her aunt, Lady Tufton, was married three times. She died the year after her niece's wedding, leaving £260 in her will to the parish of Ware, 'the interest to be applied in coats to six poor men and gowns to six poor women, once every two years, and in teaching four boys and four girls to read and write and say the catechism'. Her gravestone in St. Mary's Church in Ware lies next to that of Elizabeth Buckeridge's younger sister who died at 16. The young lad from Cornwall had done well, and no doubt he knew it. But the benefits of the marriage were not entirely one-sided: Ralph was to prove his own value both in financial and personal terms over succeeding years.

DIARY
April 10 1722

We are now the possessors of the most delightful house, not a stone's throw from General Wade's, with a garden. There has been local difficulty with this project, for the land for the garden has been taken from the bowling green beside the Abbey, and there was much objection to it from those who believe that to thus put an end to Smock-Racing, Pig Racing, playing at Foot-Ball – as well as Grinning, Staring, Scolding, eating hot Furmety, Laughing, Whistling, and Jigging upon the stage for rings, shorts, smocks, hats etc., is not Progress – which undoubtedly it is, in my plain opinion. Besides, General Wade has done much to clear the Abbey, so that the old saying is hardly true any more –

"The citizens of Bath, with vast delight, to hide their noble church from vulgar sight, surround its venerable sides with shops, and decorate its sides with chimney tops". People may now get from the churchyard to the Grove and the odious pile of buildings which disfigures the north front of the Abbey is now much diminished.

Letter from Ralph Allen to Anthony Buckeridge, brother-in-law
March 6 1724

My Dear Anthony,

I do believe we can now see our way clear to the investment of which we so recently spoke. Mr Hobbs is organising a stock company of thirty-two shares to develop the Avon as a navigable river passage between Bath and Bristol. He is a merchant of much experience and despite so much opposition – I declare I have never heard so much dissension among landowners and farmers (all of whom have a real fear of imported goods affecting their corn, butter and whatever else), the breeders of pack horses (who of course would lose much of their trade should the river be used for transport) mill owners, market traders, innkeepers – worst of them all being the colliers, who have made threats against us, for they know only too well that the arrival of excellent Shropshire coal by river will affect their prices.

However all of this will be for nought, I am sure, and I therefore suggest that you join me in purchasing a share of the company – I am to buy one, also my father and brother. Mr Hobbs has also suggested that I take the post of one of three treasurers, so you see your money will be well cared for. As you know, I have an idea for acquiring the stone quarries on Combe Down – and when one contemplates the transportation of stone, well, you will see that water transport is undoubtedly the answer.

Yours affectionately,
Ralph

It was a shrewd move. Hitherto all goods had been carried by road between Bath and Bristol, and the navigable river passage had long been proposed. For Ralph Allen it was indeed a necessity if he was to open up the stone quarries.

The stone quarries, or mines, were sometimes very high, the pillars
of limestone giving the name 'The Cathedral' to this one.

DIARY
May 10 1725

Yesterday we walked up on the Down above Widcombe, a most pleasant place of sheep pastures and quite marvellous views to all points of the compass. The air is so fresh and good there. It was remarkable level, yet very stony underfoot, and large blocks of stone from local quarrying lay all round, in such a confused manner as though they had been tumbled there by some ancient gods. The stone is used for breaking, chiefly for road making. Yet there is some mining for the stone that lies under the ground, for all the world like mining for coal: the stone comes up quite yellow, and then weathers pale grey and amber in the light. These stone quarries provide some good freestone for building, dressed at the quarry site by free masons ready for construction of the buildings by rough masons. I spoke to some of the owners of these quarries, one James Allen, William Bliss and Milo Smith.

This Bath stone is not much sold beyond Combe Down, and is not cheap, the cost of labour and transportation being very high. Yet it is good stone. I believe it as good as any from Caen or Dorset. I have it in my mind to invest in it.

Which, indeed, he did. In 1726 he bought extensive land on Combe Down from the owner, Mary Wiltshire, and next year purchased the rights of the first of the stone quarries. But not everything could go according to his plans.

DIARY
December 20 1725

A wretched Christmas. Little George died two nights ago. It makes hollow all the successes of this past year. It has been otherwise so happy for us. But what matters it to be a Freeman of the City, or an elected Councillor, or to see business flourish, all of which have given us such reward this summer, if there is no one to come after us, no child for whom to strive.

There is no evidence that Ralph Allen ever had another child. Nevertheless several nephews and nieces assuaged a little of his loss. He was close to his wife's family too. Her brother Anthony and his wife Sarah had two surviving children of whom he was to become very fond. But most of his energy was channelled into his increasingly formidable business empire.

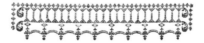

Letter from Ralph Allen to Anthony Buckeridge
June 19 1726

My Dear Anthony,

My plans concerning the stone quarries at Combe Down are going apace, and I have had another fortunate encounter with the architect John Wood. He is a young man of energy and imagination and indeed a fiery spirit, and I would be glad of any information you might have regarding him, since I understand he has had some financial difficulty with some work on the Cavendish estate in London. Tho born in Bath, I believe the son of a local builder, he has worked at Bramham Park in Yorkshire as well as in London, and is now employed by the Duke of Chandos on the restoration of St John's Hospital here in Bath. It is to be lodging houses for visitors.

Mr Wood has some strange ideas about the origins of classical architecture, concerned with King Bladud and the meaning of freemasonry. The stone circle at Stanton Drew, not far from Bath, intrigues him, and he believes it has some meaning associated with the Druids. It might sound a trifle odd, but his ideas are very beguiling, and he has such enthusiasm and so swift a hand at sketching out his ideas that I intend to employ him on designing some alterations to my house.. He has studied the Italian architects Palladio and Leoni and has acquainted me with the volumes of Colen Campbell, an architect whom he appears to regard with great admiration albeit rivalry. These volumes are entitled Vitruvius Britannicus or The British Architect. I understand Mr Campbell has found a new patron in Lord Burlington. Advise me of any knowledge you may have of Mr Wood so that I may with confidence commission him to attend to my house.

Yours etc. Ralph

There is no evidence that Ralph Allen was a freemason himself.

Letter from Ralph Allen to John Wood, Architect
May 14 1727

Sir

Since you are to be at Bramham for a month or two, I thought I should write to let you know that I have now completed the purchase of land at Combe Down from Mary Wiltshire, including the deep combe that runs down to the river. I am also well advanced in the purchase of quarries from Milo Smith of Widcombe and Thomas Greenway of Bath. Mr Smith is not yet satisfied with the terms but I am persuaded we will in the end come to an agreement. Mr Greenway is one of the finest stonecutters in Bath and I am very glad of his assistance.

John Wood the Elder, who had a vision of Bath as a great
Roman city

I say quarries; but these are, rather, stone mines. There is a stratum of limestone at the top, about four feet deep, full of tiny shells, with another stratum below, and even below that, in the fourth of which is much crystalline spar, glittering in the lamplight. But it is the fifth stratum, perhaps twenty or more feet below the surface of the ground, that provides the stone we seek. Cut and laid in the air for hardening, it is good for ornaments, but also as durable, beautiful freestone for building, although it has no reputation.

The difficulty will be in the transporting of the stone from the quarry to my river wharf at Widcombe, it is something under two miles distant and four hundred feet below the Down. The gradient is about one in 10. One block of stone may weigh as much as four tons. Horses wind the loads to the surface up the sloping shafts into the yards, but it is no wonder that there has been little work for the masons and stonedressers, so hard is it to get the stone to the yard in good enough blocks for the masons to work upon it, at least to make it at all economical. However I have been in correspondence with Mr John Padmore of Bristol, an engineer, who has a natural genius for mechanics. We are fast coming upon the solution.

I am determined that a railway – that is to say, such a road between the summit of the hill and the river as the gentlemen of the North of England have made between the collieries and the River Tyne. It should reduce the price to half that of carrying the stone down in common wagons.

The wagons are to be of oak, some 13 feet long, with detachable sides and spoked cast iron wheels, running on oak rails. All four wheels of the wagons have on the inner side a flange, which keeps the wagon between those wooden timbers. A brakesman will control the descent by means of a wooden lever known as a jig pole, the two rear wheels being braked by square wooden blocks attached to one end of these levers. At the other end the levers are held down by chains attached to pulleys, turned by a ratchet and pawl device. The front wheels are braked – or, to be more accurate – locked, by two square bars, one for each wheel, which may be independently operated from the rear of the wagon by a system of rods and levers. On level ground the wagons will be hauled by horses, two or three for fully-laden ones, and perhaps one or two for the unladen, which must make the return uphill to Combe Down.

Mr Padmore also has worked upon the design of cranes both for the quarries at Combe Down and the Dolemeads wharf at Widcombe.

Mr Richard Jones is now my Clerk of Works at Combe Down, and he oversees the quarrymasters, but I have it in my mind to build some houses for the men to assure myself, and them, of some security of employment. Therefore I would ask you to think on some plans for such houses close to the quarries, and also for others close to the stone yard and wharf on the river at Widcombe.

Yours etc
Ralph Allen

1.
Ralph Allen, painted by William Hoare in 1742. The portrait is
in the collection of the Royal National Hospital for Rheumatic
Diseases in Bath, founded by Allen and fellow 'Bath worthies'.
(*Bath in Time - Bath Royal National Hospital for Rheumatic Diseases*)

2.

Watercolours by Thomas Robins, painted in the 1750s, and showing (top) Allen's wharf at Widcombe, looking south from South Parade on the River Avon and (below) Prior Park. Capability Brown later altered the garden and removed the cascade.

(V&A Images, Victoria and Albert Museum, London)

3.

The King's Bath
"very large, and the hot springs bubble up so fast and so strong
they must be hot against the bottoms of one's feet..."

4.

Richard 'Beau' Nash ruled Bath as Master of Ceremonies. Even the aristocracy obeyed his diktats: he would cheerfully reprimand a duchess if she refused a country dance when asked.

5.
Sally Lunn was the creator of a brioche-like bun, and this house, where she first baked it in the 17th century is reputed to be the oldest in Bath. The bun is still baked to the original recipe and sold here at Sally Lunn's House.

6.
General Wade, Allen's early benefactor, lived in the Abbey Church Yard at No.14. It was built in about 1720, before John Wood, possibly by Thomas Greenway.

7.
The White Hart in Widcombe, an old coaching inn, alongside
which Ralph Allen built a terrace of workers' cottages - saved
from demolition in the 1960s.

8.
Now tucked almost out of sight off Parade Gardens, Ralph Allen's
town house was once also the post office.

Ralph Allen's railway not only made his stone so competitive in price that he was able to buy out his competitors, but was for a time a local wonder. Crowds came to marvel at it. It began at what is now the newsagent's in Combe Down, at the end of The Avenue, where stone was loaded on to the carriages. Wheels on the newsagent's wall commemorate the building's later identity as the Carriage Inn. The railway ended at what was then the stone yard in Widcombe, close to the wharf in Dolemeads Meadow beside the Avon. What is now Ralph Allen's Drive was a private road until early last century, with gates across it.

Ten years later Sir John Evelyn visited Bath, and wrote in his diary:

> "I went one morning to Mr Allen the Postmaster's great stone quarry, and the new house he is building near it, upon one of the hills about a mile from the town, the stone works easier than wood when first cut out of the quarry but hardens they say by the weather, 'tis conveyed in a very clever manner down to the town upon carriages with low broad wheels covered with iron which run upon a wooden frame made the length of the hill, so that when the machine is set agoing it runs down the hill without any help, one man behind to steer it, and in this manner above three tons of stone are carried down at one load."

The houses built for the quarrymen in Combe Down were once known as the 'Old Rank', before a later landowner gave his name, de Montalt, to the perfect vernacular terrace of houses with Richard Jones's Dial House in the centre.

Thomas Greenway, the master mason from whom Ralph Allen bought one of the quarries, was also an architect of considerable talent. Marshall Wade's house may have been designed by him, as were four houses which now form parts of the present Theatre Royal and Garrick's Head pub. One of them was Beau Nash's first house.

DIARY
July 14 1727

The Postmasters General, Edward Carteret and Edward Harrison, with, as I judged, the greatest readiness, eight days ago signed a contract with me for another seven years. It is on the same terms as before, save some more improvement on the Dover and Yarmouth roads. I am confident that this means the surplus will be considerable, and enable me to share a large portion of the proceeds with my brother – Philip is the best servant any man could have and it pleases me greatly that he should seem to be content in working with me on these many enterprises.

Life is most pleasurable at present in the City. We have celebrated the accession of King George II with much festivity, and we are now to plan more such celebrations for his birthday in November. Also there has been great excitement over the discovery of a life-size bronze head of a Roman goddess. It was found in a great trench dug for a new sewer along Stall Street, only two days past. It is believed to be the head of Minerva. She has most elegantly braided hair, once gilded, as no doubt the whole statue once was. Mr Wood is most taken with it, tho so far there are no other finds.

The alterations to our house are now complete: Mr Wood has added another storey, an ornamental pediment, and four pilasters with Corinthian capitals. It is quite magnificent – as Mr Wood himself declares – and no doubt a splendid advertisement for his skills. Also we now have sufficient accommodation for the cross-posts branch of the business, the local postal business being carried on in the basement and first storey while my brother Philip now may take residence in the upper portion. From my house a terraced walk leads down to Harrison's Walks and the Grove, and we have a fine view of the bare down above the river meadows.

The head of Minerva, probably once part of a statue in the Roman temple, is today in the Roman Baths Museum.

Letter from John Wood to Ralph Allen
May 10 1728

Sir

I have done with them all. Yesterday I was at Salter's Hall in the City of London, as you know, for the public meeting of the Governors of Greenwich Hospital, to present to them our Bath stone and to persuade them of its virtues and superiority over Portland stone, which they made clear they preferred from the outset. Also there, of course, was the Architect, Mr Colin Campbell, author of Vitruvius Britannicus. I had anticipated some attack and had caused a Bath mason to accompany me with a sample of each sort of stone, Bath and Portland. The blocks of stone were not identified.

The Governors ordered the patterns to be laid on the table before them. They were entirely candid in their opinions of Bath stone: 'unable to bear any weight, of a coarse texture, bad colour and almost as dear as Portland stone in any case for a public work in or near London'. I even heard someone repeat the calumny about Bath stone being like Cheshire Cheese, 'liable to breed maggots that would soon devour it'. So Mr Campbell made his choice of the samples of stone - which, as I have said, were unlabelled. And what did he choose? Why, the most superior – Bath stone. Was this not a notorious proof of his earlier partiality? Yet he was not to be moved, declaring it not to be a perfect example. Nor would the Governors admit defeat upon this point. Indeed, they simply used it as a way of lowering the price of the Portland Stone, saying that they would still prefer the well-tried material with which they were familiar, but that since the Bath Stone was available at such a saving in money, then they would contract for the Portland at a lower price than that previously paid.

Yours etc. John Wood

Letter from Ralph Allen to John Wood
May 17 1728

My Dear Wood,

I can only say that this setback must not deter us: indeed, I believe it to be a sign that we should take up the challenge of demonstrating the superiority, the beauty and durability of Bath Stone. There will be other contracts. And I have the idea for a house near the Combe Down quarries, a house which will exhibit the virtues of Bath Stone to much greater advantage, and in much greater variety of uses, than has ever appeared in any other structure. It will be prove our point, and set the truth in stone itself."

Yours with resolution,
Ralph Allen

There was, indeed, another contract. Two years later Ralph was asked to supply Bath stone for St Bartholomew's Hospital in London, the architect being Sir James Gibbs. Nevertheless it was never to be a particularly lucrative or satisfying project. Despite the successful opening of the river route to Bristol, transporting the Bath Stone by ship from Bristol to London was always fraught with problems, not just because of the hazards of weather and sea, but war.

Yet locally, Bath Stone was now being widely used, and at the end of 1728 John Wood broke ground for the first of his houses in Queen Square. It was to be his first great achievement, part of his vision of transforming Bath from a mediaeval town into a beautiful and spacious City. He might have been disappointed with Colin Campbell for not upholding his choice of Bath stone for Greenwich Hospital, but they shared a love of the principles of the same Italian architect, Andrea Palladio.

DIARY
March 21 1729

I have today been to have my portrait painted by Mr Van Diest, whom General Wade has asked to paint portraits of the Mayor and each of the Aldermen at his own expense, to be hung in the Guildhall, as a token of his gratitude to the men who had honored him with election to Parliament. I dare to say that it will be an excellent likeness, and I like Mr Van Diest's suggestion that he add a touch of stone column to the picture. As I am not an Alderman, but a Councilman, it is a singular honour, and I cannot say I am not proud of it.

Yesterday I rode up to Combe Down to meet Mr Jones and inspect the work in the quarries, and to see what progress is made on the roads and new houses for the quarrymen. The day was very pleasant, a cool breeze, and the view across to the Wiltshire Downs above Westbury and I dare say as far as Salisbury Plain was quite exceptionally fine. The houses are now roofed, not with thatch or slate but flat slabs of stone, as it were large shingles, a style I think particularly suited to these houses. I do think Mr Wood has made an excellent work of them.

I have of late been sorely tried by some of the postmasters, like those at Worcester and Bewdley who by private agreement have been encouraging their postboys to exchange mails at an alehouse on the road, thus sparing themselves the trouble of opening the bags properly in both offices at recorded hours. Indeed, they leave most of their work to the unsupervised, unbonded postboys. It is my continual effort to try to redress such abuses, albeit with tenderness and caution. The postal delivery benefits commerce and strengthens trade – letters are trade. If it also leads to exchanges of affection and of news, of elegance of handwriting and grace of expression, then that is even more pleasing.

A post-boy carrying the mail to the next 'stage', or post office.

DIARY
February 19 1732

Philip's marriage to Jane Bennet, sister of Philip Bennet of Widcombe House, was a very happy occasion. They were married at Claverton. I am truly happy for him, and indeed for myself, that he has so well established himself in society. They will live at Widcombe. God grant that they will have a child of their own, for I doubt that such a gift will ever be mine. Yet I have the cares of children now: my Cornish niece and nephew, sadly orphaned after the death of my sister Elizabeth last November, are come to visit from St Blazey. Gertrude (Gatty) Tucker is eight, William (Billy) seven. I have added their names to the pew book in St James's Church so they too will have a place in Bath. I have given Billy's name as Allen – there is another William Tucker so it will avoid any confusion – and it pleases me, for he and Gatty are a bright and charming pair.

Philip Allen and his wife Jane had a daughter, Molly, in 1734. Philip's wife Jane was part of a higher social stratum from the Allens, who while occupying their now elegant house in Bath still combined it with the city's Post Office. The marriage marked the family's rise. The Bennets at Widcombe occupied one of the most charming new houses in the area, Widcombe Manor, and Philip Allen's newly acquired brother in law was to be elected a Member of Parliament later that year. And in December of 1734 William, Prince of Orange, came to Bath for seven weeks, twice visiting Ralph's stone quarries. He also admired John Wood's partly completed Queen Square. Ralph Allen was now one of the city's leading residents.

In September Anthony Buckeridge, Mrs Allen's brother, suddenly died. His daughter Elizabeth was only three months old. He had named Ralph Allen as 'Guardian or Trustee' for his three surviving children, and his widow Ann depended on Allen for advice and help in the years ahead.

Letter from Ralph Allen to Ann Buckeridge, sister-in-law
November 4 1734

Dear Sister-in-law

I hope you have recovered from your attack of the colic, no doubt a result of your grieving, and that the children are able to give you some comfort. I myself have been suffering from some lowness of spirits and disorder of health in recent weeks, tho to be sure this past year has been one of much celebration in the City, with comings and goings of all manner of people – we have had Lords Chesterfield and Burlington, Mr Swift, and John Gay. We had a special performance of his Beggar's Opera, and although of course many talk of it being a satire of Sir Robert Walpole and his government, indeed of society, it is nevertheless a play of such diverting amusement and drama that it stands entirely by itself. Polly Peachum and MacHeath represent the highwayman Jonathan Wild, and the thief Jack Sheppard, but I can see that the satire goes beyond these.

I have recently made the acquaintance in particular of Mr Alexander Pope, who came to Bath with Lord Bolingbroke, and was also accompanied by his friend Mrs Martha Blount. He is undoubtedly small and somewhat deformed but of so lively a wit and sharp an intellect that the encounter was especially pleasing. He is also a great gardener and I was able to talk of my plans for the new house on the hillside above Widcombe, which are now taking shape not only in my mind. However I have decided that while those plans come to fruition, we shall remove in the meantime to Widcombe, leaving the Post Office here of course in Lilliput Alley, where my brother Philip will remain. The city is full of crowds and we are a little too close to the baths and gaming rooms, and in any case there is a great deal more business being done at the Post Office, and a multitude of postboys, posthorses and visitors seeking their mail. A little peace and quiet will do us no harm.

Among the crowds here has been the Princess of Amelia, whose sister has so recently married William, Prince of Orange. He brought his bride to Bath in April and Mr Richard Nash has erected a thirty foot tall obelisk in what is now to be called the 'Orange' Grove. I am not too modest to tell you also that a Miss Mary Chandler has published a poem dedicated to Princess Amelia, in which she makes reference to myself, and indeed to my plans for the new house in the most extravagant terms. I enclose a copy of the poem, and you may make of it what you will, but I cannot but admit that I find it most humbling.

Your affectionate
Ralph

Mary Chandler's poem *A Description of Bath* became very well known, often reprinted and quoted. It describes Ralph Allen as:

Virtue's Exemplar in degenerate days,
All who love Virtue, love to speak your Praise:
You chide the Muse that dares your Virtues own,
And, veiled with Modesty, would live unknown.

Letter from Ralph Allen to Ann Buckeridge
January 24 1736

Dear Sister-in-law

I thank God that I am now much recovered from my late relapse, but my wife has been very ill for some time and still continues very weak. I have been absent thro sickness from several meetings of the City council. The construction of my estate at Widcombe, Prior Park, goes ahead, and life here out of the City is of benefit to us all. I was much delighted with the publication of Mr Pope's 'Letters' last summer, and have suggested to him that I pay for a new, authentic edition. In return he assures me he will advise me on the landscaping work to be done at Prior Park. I hope to visit him at Twickenham in the spring.

Your affectionate
Ralph

Elizabeth Allen, Ann Buckeridge's sister-in-law, died some weeks later. There is no record of her burial in any of the Bath parishes and it is probable that she was buried in her family ground at Ware.

Letter from Ralph Allen to Alexander Pope
September 20 1736

Sir

I mentioned in my last that I have had some troublesome family concerns, tho all seems improving now with the health of Mrs Buckeridge and young Lewis. I have also had concerns with the new wing for St Bartholomew's Hospital, as you know, but I am glad that the work occasioned my last visit to you in London and I would wish to thank you for your hospitality. Work goes ahead at Prior Park, tho so far only the large westward offices, the stables, granaries, pigeon house etc., are under construction.

There has been a great new map of the City published by Mr Leake, the bookseller, copied from the original survey by John Wood, and annotated by him with certain attractions of Bath – among them my crane for loading the stone on to barges, which he calls a 'Masterpiece of Mechanism' – also he advertises the stone with a great deal of energy and cheerful spirit.

I look forward with much impatience to the publication of the new edition of the Letters, and also to your returning my two visits to you this year..."

Yours etc
Allen

Alexander Pope was already a famous poet, satirist and writer when he met Ralph Allen. It was perhaps an unlikely friendship that grew between them, but Pope evidently found Allen's modesty – and wealth – appealing, and they undoubtedly shared a love of beauty in both architecture, literature and gardens. Pope was a political meddler, and often manipulative, but Allen never took his bait: perhaps his practical, balanced outlook also attracted the often arrogant writer. And Allen's generosity and love of books was something that linked him to many writers of the day, although his own writing never rose above the practical and precise. He was also a very generous friend and host, even when severely tried by Pope's frequent selfishness – or at least, when the second Mrs Allen was severely tried.

Letter from Alexander Pope to Ralph Allen
May 14 1736

My Dear Allen
Now that the Letters are issued, I would be
honoured if you would accept a special copy of the
work printed on very fine royal paper quarto size,
and, if you will, I would also like to present such
a copy of General Wade and indeed to Mrs Allen.
Also, tho I am a trifle late in doing so but would
very much wish to congratulate you on your recent
marriage.

Yours etc
Pope

Ralph Allen had married Elizabeth Holder on March 24,
1737, at the new and much admired church of St Martin-
in-the-Fields in London. The architect of St Martin-in-the-
Fields was James Gibb, with whom Ralph had worked on
the building of St Bartholomew's Hospital. Ralph was
forty-three when he married for the second time, his bride
thirty-nine. Her father owned the beautiful old Hampton
Manor House at Bathampton, where she had lived before
her marriage. There was, as it happened, good Bath freestone
to be quarried at Bathampton, and Allen was not slow to
acquire the rights to it.

Elizabeth Holder gives the impression of being an
intelligent and sensible woman, and some months after their
marriage Ralph wrote a letter to the friend and clergyman
who had married them, expressing his happiness. "Her
whole employment," he said, "has been in her duty to a
supreme being and an uninterrupted endeavour to heighten
my happiness."

DIARY
December 20 1737

Much business at present to do with the proposed new Bath General Hospital, of which I became a Governor earlier this year. It is only now, after many years, that the proposal has reached the stage of planning some solid form. Mr Nash was one of its earliest supporters. I have already bound myself to supply, free of expense, all wrought free stones, paving stones, wall stones and lime, for the building, and subscriptions have begun to pour into the fund. John Wood is already working on the designs and I hope we should lay the cornerstone by the summer of next year. I am much exercised by making this known by both within the City and beyond, for there is a scurrilous poem doing the rounds at present which is doing great harm to all. The author is unknown; I only wish I knew who might be writing such stuff. He speaks of murderous physicians, greedy apothecries, filthy baths... I hardly bear to quote:

> *"....Streets ne'er clean.*
> *A trifling Mayor; a squabbling Corporation;*
> *A sharking People, scum of all the Nation..."*

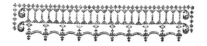

Letter from Alexander Pope to Ralph Allen
April 28 1738

Dear Allen

...Pray tell me if you have any objection to my putting your name into a poem of mine, (incidentally, not at all going out of the way for it) provided I say something of you which most people would take ill, for example, that you are no man of high birth or quality?   You must be perfectly free with me on this, as on any, nay on every, other occasion.

Yours etc
Pope

DIARY
May 25 1738

I received today Mr Pope's poem, One Thousand Seven Hundred and Thirty Eight, in which there is a reference to me. It is, I believe, a satirical work that honours the Prince of Wales and condemns Sir Robert Walpole, and perhaps Mr Pope considers that I might therefore share his views on politics, but I do not, and indeed must not, since he favours the Opposition and I serve the Government in the form of the Postmasters General.   The passage in which my name appears is one I find not altogether to my liking –

"Let low-born Allen, with an awkward Shame,
Do good by stealth, and blush to find it Fame…"

It may be true that I would rather my acts of charity were not made for show or any kind of fame, but tho I would not protest too much, I am unhappy about the phrase 'low-born Allen'. My family had no land or great estates, but that phrase…well, for my part, I might say 'humble', for indeed I have never made pretence of any other origin, but 'low-born' smells of something less than I believe I am. I will have to ask him to alter it. It irks me to see it there.

Pope did change the phrase 'low-born' to 'humble'.

DIARY
July 6 1738

Today laid the cornerstone of the new Bath Hospital, the ceremony performed by the Hon. William Pulteney. Now perhaps we can pursue the building work, and cease so much talk, for I weary of all the meetings with such men as Mr Nash, let alone the physicians and those who feel that they must have a say. At least I can enjoy the company of Dr Oliver. Perhaps our Cornish origins form a bond of friendship between us - besides, he is always in good spirits and humour. During the excavations Mr Wood uncovered part of a Roman building. He was delighted with this find and has meticulously recorded it, believing it to be part of the ancient praetorium, the centre of a great Roman town and he says it justifies his vision.

Dr William Oliver (of the famous Bath Oliver biscuits) was one of Ralph Allen's expanding circle of friends as well as an active colleague on the board of the Bath Hospital. They shared a Cornish background and were both interested in books, art and architecture. Oliver was a cheerful and civilised character who made no secret of his pleasure in having the opportunity to share the company of one whom many considered the greatest poet and writer in England, Alexander Pope. His cousin, William Borlase, was also a member of the circle of friends: an Oxford graduate and country clergyman, he was fascinated by geology and helped to create Pope's celebrated grotto at this villa in Twickenham.

August 17 1738

I have arranged for eight bottles of Bath water
to be despatched weekly to Twickenham for the
benefit of Mr Pope's guest, Lord Bolingbroke.

November 8 1738

We have today received thanks from Mr Pope for
the guinea hens, oil, wine and the Bristol water.
He has requested six stone urns from me. I shall
send Biggs as the mason to do the stonework at
Twickenham.

March 22 1739

A surprise gift from Mr Pope: a puppy, descendant
of his dog Bounce – a Great Dane, and so young it
can but just lap milk.

April 14 1739

Amazing scenes in Bath this past week. The Rev
John Wesley has visited on horseback from Bristol
to save our souls... Some thousand people gathered
to hear him offer the free grace of God – more the
next day, with much faintings and fits to mark the
departure of Satan from the poor creatures. Mr
Nash made an attempt to silence him, for fear that
the Rev Wesley would distress those who wish
simply to go about their pleasures in Bath, and
the crowds are causing damage, hysteria and even
larceny, but the preacher rather silenced Mr Nash.
However I suspect the excitement will not endure,

and several fine gay jokers from the Pump Room joined in the throng for the sport of it, and in doing so made game of it. For myself, I have enough to be busy with without asking for a thunderbolt to save my soul.

Alexander Pope spent Christmas with the Allens at their house in Widcombe. He was well looked after by Mrs Allen – she even found him a special little green chair to fit his small frame. He wrote to his friend William Fortescue:

Letter from Alexander Pope to William Fortescue
January 8 1740

...Mr Allen suffers no misery near him. Whoever is lame, or any way disabled, he gives weekly allowances to the wife or children: besides large supplies of other kinds to the Poor. God made this man rich, to shame the great; and wise, to humble the learned. I envy none of you in Town the honours you may have received at court, or from the higher powers: I have passed this Christmas with the most noble man of England.

Yours etc
Pope

Letter from Dr William Oliver to the Rev William Borlase
January 14 1740

Mr Pope is the freest, humblest, most entertaining creature you ever met with; he has sojourned these two months with our great countryman, Mr Allen, at his country house. They are extremely happy in each other; the one feeling great joy in the good heart, and strong sense of his truly generous host, while the house, with the most pleasing attention, drinks in rivers of knowledge continually flowing from the lips of his delightful stranger. They are much alone, and quite happy in each other, but they are so kind as to say that I do not interrupt them when I make a third for an hour or two, which I believe you will not imagine to be very seldom. Mr Pope has been in some ill health, and has taken the waters at Bristol, then at Bath, and also at the newly discovered spring in Lyncombe near the Allen's home. I believe Mr Pope finds the Allens' home a most comfortable place, for they allow him all privacy and freedom, and their style of living is not grand nor crowded with visitors. The puppy is charming.

Yours ever
Dr William Oliver

At about this time Ralph Allen first met Henry Fielding, a young impecunious playwright who was one of a group of satirical writers of the time.   The object of their venom was Sir Robert Walpole, Britain's first prime minister, and so powerful not only in the then Whig government but in the country as a whole that he was generally referred to as 'The Great Man'.   Indeed, Fielding might have been successful as a playwright had Walpole not brought in censorship of plays and theatres in 1737. Fielding then went into the law in an effort to support his wife and children, and as a barrister on the west circuit he may have first met Ralph Allen in Bristol or Bath. It may have been earlier, since Fielding eloped with Charlotte Cradock in 1734 and they were married in Charlcombe on the edge of Bath; also his sister Sarah settled in the city not long afterwards. What is pretty clear is that they became friends, despite the fact that Fielding loathed Walpole's government and Ralph Allen was a servant of it. Certainly Allen was in a position to help Fielding in practical and financial ways.

Fielding may have been spurred into writing novels by the publication of *Pamela: or, Virtue Rewarded.* It was by a 51 year old printer called Samuel Richardson. It was an immediate success, and both Pope and Allen found it delightful and admirable.

DIARY
May 24 1741

So at last we are here, at Prior Park. It has been seven years in the planning and 'tis not yet finished – the east wing remains to complete – but the house itself is all but done. The lawns, the trees, are made, and flourish. Mr Wood attempted to inflict much ornamentation on it but I have kept it as plain as possible within the greatness and magnificence of its size, its views, its setting – and most of all, perhaps, its stone. It curves, rather than stands square on the hillside. I know of no other such villa with this eccentricity. Mr Wood planned it as three sides of a duodecagon, describing the natural terraces of the hill on which it is set as 'sitting above one another, like the stages between the seats of a Roman theatre'. The whole is constructed of blocks of freestone in equal courses, the upper storeys resting on fine basement arches, the whole kept firm and secure by 800 tons of large blocks of stone buried as a foundation on this ledge that overlooks the city. It is true that John Norris wrote in his Treatise on Humility that "humility lives at the bottom of the hill", but I believe that this house will prove an exception to that rule.

The chief rooms are pale freestone, the walls ornamented with all manner of delicate carving, the gallery upstairs being 90 feet long with a ceiling 20 feet high, where I intend to make a 'secret' library – the shelves being covered by doors on which the philosophers, etc, will be painted. Mr Pope has ideas for certain statues to place here. In the blue parlour we have put a portrait of General Wade, and in the dining room a picture I have always had a fancy for, since it depicts 'The Fable of the Fowls plucking the Crow of his borrow'd feathers'. The house is grand, and will, I think, persuade any doubter that Bath stone is unparalleled in beauty and durability; yet I hope that it offers also a place for tranquillity, for contemplation, and for civilised intercourse between people of like minds and good conversation. Some say that Bath is increasingly a centre of racket and dissipation with a deal of gossip and intrigue, that there is little bond of union amongst the various classes that visit the City. Well, that may be, but still I find the bookshops full, and many lectures and displays for the more cultured mind, and perhaps 'tis in the view of the beholder to see such vulgarity. Nevertheless I will hope to make Prior Park a place to cultivate the exercise of those graces which adorn the sociable life.

The stables are very fine, with six recessed stalls on every side, arched and lined with dressed stone, and a porte cochère for carriages. Little Gatty says I treat my horses like gentlemen, and I fancy she is right in it; but so much do we depend upon them, and so generously and willingly do they labour for us, that I can only think they deserve no less. It is sad that Wood and I should have fallen out over the alterations and ornamentation to this west wing, and perhaps we both made too much of it, but I have determined that Richard Jones shall complete the building to Mr Wood's designs. Since

Mr Wood is exceptionally busy at present there is no serious rift between us – nothing that cannot be mended, at any rate, for we are allies and friends at bottom.

I should mention the park, it being a matter of continuing pleasure and absorption. We have made it something between the Roman, that is, the Palladian ideal, according to Mr Wood, and the new ideas for pleasant lawns, clumps of trees and winding rivers and paths. Already we have planted elms and many thousands of fir trees on the Down above.

In 1742 Daniel Defoe published the *Tour Thro the Whole Island of Great Britain* in which Prior Park, along with Ralph Allen's quarries, wharf and railway, were enthusiastically described – as it happened, by the author of *Pamela*, Samuel Richardson, one of the contributors to the book. Bath Stone was said to be not only handsome, as all the new buildings demonstrated, but cheap. There was a long paragraph on the 'hot, milky, soft, salutiferous Beverage, called Bath Water' – but also a good deal about the city's narrowness of spirit, the greed of its citizens and its indifference to the maintenance of the baths.

Defoe himself later described the gardens that spread below Prior Park as consisting of two terraces and two slopes, with 'winding walks made through a little coppice opening to the westward of those slopes; but all these are adorned with vases, and other ornaments, in stonework; and the affluence of water is so great, that it is received in three different places, after many little agreeable falls, at the head of one of which is a statue of Moses down to the knees, in an attitude expressive of the admiration he must have been in after striking the Rock, and seeing the water gush out of it. The winding walks were made with great labour; and, tho no broader than for two or three to walk abreast, yet in some places they appear with little cliffs on one side, and with small precipices on the other'.

Alexander Pope greatly influenced the garden design, including the 'sham bridge' over the stream in the deep valley, and at least one grotto following the rustic style he had made fashionable with his own.

Letter from Alexander Pope to the Rev William Warburton
September 2 1741

Dear Warburton,

I am here in more leisure than I can possibly enjoy even in my own house...the worthy Man who is the Master of it invites you in the strongest terms, and is one who would treat you with love and veneration, rather than what the World calls civility and regard. He is sincerer and plainer than almost any man now in this world. If the waters of the Bath may be serviceable to your complaints, (as I believe from what you have told me of them) no opportunity can ever be better...You'll want no servant here, your room will be next to mine, and one man will serve us. Here is a Library, and a Gallery ninety foot long to walk in, and a Coach whenever you would take the air with me...Mr Allen's house (where I am, and hope you may be) is less than two miles from Bath, but his Brother the Postmaster lives at Bath, and takes care of the Letters to me.

Be pleased to go, when you arrive, to the Postmaster's house in Bath, where you shall find a Coach: and your chamber here ready aired and with all possible care. You will owe me real obligation by being made acquainted with the Master of this House; and by sharing with me, what I think one of the chief satisfactions of my Life, His Friendship.
Yours etc
Pope

The country clergyman, William Warburton, later Bishop of Gloucester, was one of Pope's closest friends and was to become one of Ralph Allen's. Self-taught, highly intelligent and ambitious, Warburton was often arrogant and prejudiced. He upset a lot of people in print, but in private he could be charming, particularly when it suited him, and it usually suited him to be charming to Allen. He collected books, as did Allen. They bequeathed their libraries to a mutual friend, Richard Hurd, another clergyman of some independent means though by no means wealthy.

With Allen's help, Richard Hurd found a 'sinecure rectory' in Yorkshire, giving him an income of £150 a year. Later he became chaplain to William Warburton, and following the deaths of both Warburton and Allen he became Bishop of Worcester. In 1782 he built the beautiful Hurd Library at the Bishop's Palace, Hartlebury Castle in Worcestershire, of which Pope's and Allen's books form the major part. Their portraits hang in the library.

DIARY
February 23 1742

So Walpole is gone. He has resigned. Carteret is now Secretary of State and the Earl of Wilmington is in Walpole's place as First Lord of the Treasury. I think there will be little effect on my work with the postal system: however, I shall remain aware of the shifts in political matters, and take my cue in consequence.

Sir Robert Walpole is known as Britain's first Prime Minister although it was not a title that was used by the then First Lord of the Treasury - it was regarded as an insult. He was also the first to live at 10 Downing Street. A powerful and manipulative figure, he effectively ruled the country for 21 years and only resigned after a confrontation between Britain and Spain in the Caribbean called the War of Jenkin's Ear - so called because an English sea captain claimed the Spanish had cut off his ear. That small and lamentable war became part of a greater one, the War of the Austrian Succession, which saw Britain once more in conflict in France. Walpole was widely regarded as corrupt, and in the end saw his authority diminish in the face of public hostility.

DIARY
April 3 1742

I have been much diverted from events of state by the publication of a new novel, 'The History of the Adventures of Joseph Andrews'. Anonymous it may be, but the author is Mr Fielding, and he has told me that there are references to myself as a Commoner raised higher above the Multitude by superior talents... A Master of Affability. Indeed, he has Joseph himself speak of my 'stately house too, which the Squire likes very well; but his Charity is seen farther than his House, tho it stands on a Hill, ay, and brings him more Honour.' It would give me pleasure even were these references in some dry and otherwise unimportant work, but this is Mr Fielding's first novel, and not only I, but many, regard it as full of life and honesty – not to say entertainment.

DIARY
November 5 1742

Such a year it has been. It began with Walpole's departure, and has ended with my own elevation to Mayor of Bath. I celebrated my half century: and I have also been chosen as President of the new Bath General Hospital, as successor to General Wade. Last month Mr Warburton preached a sermon in the Abbey to promote, as he said, "the charity and subscription towards the General Hospital", which indeed has been of great benefit, and which he dedicated to myself and other Governors of the institution. I may say that I am not much older than Mr Warburton, yet he has paid particular attention to Miss Gatty, who is just fifteen years old, and Elizabeth has remarked that 'there is something in it'. I wish she would not have such fancies.

Also we have seen the publication of Mr Wood's 'Essay Towards a Description of the City of Bath'. He writes of his vision to recreate it as a city to 'vie with the famous City of Vicenza, in Italy, when in its highest Pitch of Glory, by the excellent Art of the celebrated Andrea Palladio'. Of course, as is his way, he castigates the baths: he describes the walls of the pools as encrusted with dirt and nastiness. There is some truth in his complaint and for that I am glad indeed that I am not mentioned in his Essay, tho others are.

I agree with Mr Wood about the separation of the masons' trade in the city. As he says, the free masons who cut and shape the stone at the quarry have their skills undermined by those of the rough masons, who so often handle the stone carelessly in the construction with it. Which indeed is why I like to send my own masons along with any stone I sell, to oversee its use.

However, as to Mr Wood's notions of antiquity and his identification of Abaris, an ancient priest of Apollo, with King Bladud, who is said to have founded Bath in 480 BC – well, I am perhaps not well versed enough in classical antiquity to give an opinion on them.

John Wood published two versions of his Essay. In the second, expanded version, seven years later, he spoke at length about Ralph Allen, his charitable work and his houses. And Mrs Allen was right about Warburton's predilection: he married the feisty Gertrude, 'Little Gatty', daughter of Ralph's late sister, less than four years later. On the death of her mother, Allen's widow, she and the ebullient clergyman would inherit Prior Park.

Letter from the Rev William Warburton to Philip Doddridge
February 16 1743

Sir

I got home a little before Christmas, after a charming philosophical retirement in a palace with Mr Pope and Mr Allen for two or three months. The gentleman I mentioned last is, I verily believe, the greatest private character that ever appeared in any age of the world. You see his munificence to the Bath Hospital. This is but a small part of his charities, and charity but a small part of his virtues. I have studied his character even maliciously, to find where his weakness lies: but have studied in vain…

Yours etc.
William Warburton

DIARY
May 9 1743

Indeed, life is sweet, tho even to write the words invites Providence to dash the cup from the lip... Yet small things have made me feel thus. The does in the deer park have had fawns, as if a gift to me. Prior Park is well established and runs smoothly now. Philip looks after the Post Office so well that much is lifted from my shoulders – tho not all. Our dear sister-in-law has married again, to Mr Ball, and seems v happy. We have many good friends, among them those of the medical profession as well as men of the Church, writers, and poets. And this summer we expect Mr Pope and Mr Warburton to spend some more time here, to which, of course, we look forward, tho Mr Pope is suffering much from asthma, and there is all the more reason that he should stay with us.

Providence must have been watching over his shoulder. What should have been an enjoyable summer turned out to be a trifle difficult. At the outset, Pope suggested that he and his friend George Arbuthnot should not stay at Prior Park at all, but at Mrs Allen's family home, the Manor House at Bathampton. It was unoccupied, but the Allens occasionally used the house, and Elizabeth Allen certainly had no intention of letting Pope move in. Ralph suggested, perhaps in conciliatory fashion, that it would be better for Pope to stay at Prior Park for the sake of his health - he could be better looked after there.

Unfortunately George Arbuthnot did not get on with William Warburton, so that was another area of tension. Worse still, a few days later Miss Martha Blount arrived, and things became even trickier. Martha Blount was an old friend – companion, perhaps mistress, soul mate – whom Pope had known since his youth. She was now 53, a devout Roman Catholic, and, it seems, quick to take offence. According to Ralph Allen there was a distinct coolness between his wife Elizabeth and the haughty Miss Blount – 'a mutual dissatisfaction'.

Much later Gertrude Tucker, who was then 16, recalled how she had heard Miss Blount come into Mr Pope's bedchamber between six and seven in the mornings – she had heard them talking – and yet at breakfast Miss Blount would ask Pope how he had rested that night, as if she hadn't seen him at all. It is very possible that Gertrude told her aunt about this apparent impropriety and that Mrs Allen was not amused - or, perhaps, and more annoyingly for Miss Blount, much entertained....

And then there was Miss Blount's insistence on using Ralph Allen's coach to go to mass in the Catholic chapel in Bath, despite his concern that as Mayor he might offend those of the Anglican faith by such a public gesture. Allen's coach was a very smart vehicle, always drawn by four richly caparisoned horses, and he was extremely proud of it. It would undoubtedly have attracted comment and probably gossip had she used it as she wished.

Whatever it was, Pope and Allen fell out over the incident, and both Pope and Miss Blount abruptly departed – separately, so as not to cause more gossip, so she stayed on at Prior Park for several more days...

Letter from Martha Blount to Alexander Pope
August 1743

I hope you are well. I am not. My spirits are quite down, tho they should not, for these people deserve so much to be despised, one should do nothing but laugh. I packed up all my things yesterday, the servants knew it, Mr and Mrs Allen never said a word, nor so much as asked me how I went or where, or when, in short from every one of them much greater inhumanity than I could conceive anybody could show. Mr Warburton takes no notice of me. Tis most wonderful, they have none of 'em named your name, nor drank your health since you went, they talk to one another without putting me at all in the conversation...I really do think, these people would shove me out, if I did not go, soon. I'll get out of it as soon, and as well as I can.

Yours etc Martha Blount

She left soon afterwards – never to return. Pope told her that he thought Mrs Allen was 'a Minx, and an impertinent one'.

DIARY
October 4 1743

I had thought the little difficulty between Elizabeth and Miss Blount might have been put behind us, but it seems there is still some awkwardness remaining. I have had a letter from Mr Pope which in some way assuages our mutual disagreement, and I have had one of my cross-post surveyors, Mr Haslem, deliver four hampers of Bristol water to Twickenham as a gesture of good will. I believe Mr Pope is also now on better terms with Mr Warburton.

However I have had other things upon my mind, and in no small way connected with Mr Pope and my desire to accommodate him. It is a year since I agreed to obtain an appointment for a certain Mr Archibald Cleland at the Bath Hospital. Now it seems there have been charges laid against him, namely that he has made medical examinations of certain patients, Mary Hook and Mary Hudson, patients indeed of doctors including Dr Oliver, without permission of the doctors, and that the examinations were of an indecent sort. The committee of the Governors has voted to suspend Mr Cleland and bar him from visiting patients until after further consideration. It has now been alleged that the two women were whores and any allegations of theirs are worthless…However, he was dismissed – only to publish 'An Appeal to the Publick' which paints all the Governors, including myself, in a very poor light.

I never liked Cleland: I wish I had not agreed to his appointment. Yet I heartily wish to find him unjustly accused, that he might have the pleasure to join in publishing his innocence. Now I am in some difficulty. Cleland is now maintaining that the management of the baths and the Hospital is unprogressive and is designed for the benefit of a small group of physicians rather than the sick. I have done as much as possible to improve the baths but it seems I get no credit... the only complaints recorded by the visiting Governors have been such things as bad beer, a broken lamp, or that the men patients sometimes go into the baths naked. More must be done, I know, but one cannot do all at once.

I have done my best to guard the honourable reputation of the Hospital. I have given stone, money, time...I have struggled to see some kind of justice done in this matter, and I wish that things had not turned out as they have. I cannot but be glad that in six days I will quit office of Mayor and have some more little peace. I have been obliged, through this business, to miss the opening of the Bristol Exchange, which I sorely regret. Reports have said how splendid the building looks, the stone pale honey in the sunlight...Yet I am not sure that I will make the journey there at present. I have such aches in my bones.

Ralph Allen was taken ill that October with what was described as an inflammatory fever, and some weeks later Elizabeth Allen caught the same infection. Fortunately by the end of the year both were recovering, and in the following March they made a trip to London. They called on Alexander Pope in Twickenham and to some extent made up their differences. Pope's health, never good, was failing, and he died two months later at the age of 56.

Pope left the major part of his library of printed books to Warburton and Ralph Allen, but in addition a bequest of £150 to Allen alone, "this being the best of my calculation, the account of what I have received from him; partly for my own, and partly for charitable purposes".

DIARY
July 12 1744

I have given the £150 left to me by Mr Pope to the Bath Hospital. I would like to believe that he is no great hand at accountancy to imply that I have done so little for him in purely financial terms over these past years. I never expected to be repaid for anything I have done for him. But if one does make some account of the cost of all the stone sent to Twickenham, the masons paid for by me, the coaches for his many journeys...well, it would add up to a little more than one hundred and fifty pounds. Those who see this sum will believe me to have been less than generous. It is an insult I will have to put behind me, so as not to sour my recollection of a man who in so many ways was the kindest I have known.

I have for some months now been subscribing to the Bath journal which first appeared in February, published by Mr Thomas Boddely here in the city. I have long said we should emulate other cities which have printed such local newspapers. It is an excellent record as well as provider of daily news and local notices. It costs two pence a copy. Mr Boddely has expressed his appreciation of the improved postal services in compiling news for the Journal.

Letter from Ralph Allen to Ann Ball (widow of Anthony Buckeridge, m Edmund Ball, again widowed)
August 29 1745

Little Gatty has become engaged to Mr Warburton. Elizabeth says she knew it would come about, but I had not believed it, tho Gatty is indeed a confident and mature young woman beyond her years, and perhaps it is no bad thing for her to have a husband before there is some indiscretion. She has a sense of humour and an ability to mix with all society, and I can see no reason why the match is not entirely desirable, although Elizabeth says that he is so much older than her – well, he is forty-six, and she eighteen; but she is older than her years, and he – well, I can recall him saying once he had not the best opinion of women, and yet he now tells me that he is offering up his freedom "to one of the finest women in England". Who can gainsay that?

In addition, young Billy (Gertrude's brother William Tucker) is to go to the Royal Naval Academy in Portsmouth. He is now seventeen, and has passed the entrance examination in mathematics. I know he will do well – he would do well anywhere.

Yours etc, Allen

In the summer of 1745 the Young Pretender, Bonnie Prince Charlie, raised his standard in Scotland. By December he had come within 130 miles of London at Derby. Everywhere people were suddenly unnerved. In Bath William Warburton preached in the Prior Park Chapel a sermon designed to deter anyone from following 'a Rabble of superstitious Ruffians, of Mountain Robbers, of half-starv'd Barbarians, with a wild and desperate Adventurer at their Head'. Ralph Allen raised a troop of a hundred men to defend the city.

The Duke of Cumberland went north to counter the Jacobite rebellion. In February 1746 news came of the Scots' retreat from Stirling.

DIARY
1746 February 10

Such celebrations! We have made a great bonfire here, the house was all lit up, with my foot soldiers firing several volleys...

On April 16 the Duke of Cumberland defeated Prince Charles and the Scots at Culloden. The defeat was followed on April 21 by more celebrations at Prior Park. A few days later Gertrude Tucker and William Warburton were married at the little church at Bathampton. Ralph Allen wrote to his sister-in-law, Ann Ball: "Gatty was married last Friday". A quiet wedding. The *Bath Journal* reported the marriage on April 28; Gertrude Tucker, it said, was 'an agreeable young lady, with a handsome fortune'.

There were other events concerning Allen's extended family. Gertrude's brother Billy was now flourishing at the Naval Academy in Portsmouth, but Lewis Buckeridge, the son of Ann Ball, Allen's first wife's sister-in-law, was something of a trial. He was now 18 and completing his studies at school. That summer he suddenly ran away to sea – or that was his intention. Allen wrote a stern letter to his mother, comparing poor Lewis (Lewy) unfavourably with Billy in terms of talent and training.

Letter from Ralph Allen to Ann Ball
June 16 1746

My Dear
I have no acquaintance with any captains in the Navy who might be persuaded to add him, without training, to their staff. I hope that on cool reflection the young man will again return to and speedily pursue his studies in that profession which he chose, and his friends think he has abilities greatly to improve in.

Your affectionate
Ralph

What did happen to Lewy is not known – but by coincidence, perhaps, later that summer among the visitors to Prior Park was Henry Fielding. He was then living in a house in Twerton, writing his novel *The History of Tom Jones, A Foundling*, and certainly dined several times at Prior Park. No doubt the subject of young Lewis and his hotheadedness in running off to seek his fortune, unlike his diligent cousin, was discussed. Indeed, Ralph Allen no doubt talked of his problems with the postboys and the postal system in general – not only is Fielding's hero Tom Jones a young runaway, but the novel also contains a lot about the misbehaviour of postboys.

Yet it was Ralph Allen himself who is portrayed in *Tom Jones* as Squire Allworthy, the kind, wealthy Somerset landowner on whose estate the foundling Tom Jones is discovered as a baby. Prior Park is recognisable as being of 'the best Grecian architecture' on the side of a hill with trees above, and a cascade of water gushing out of a rock covered with firs, falling to a lake 'at the foot of the hill, about a quarter of a mile below the house' – although from Squire Allorthy's house one can see the sea.

The portrait is often precise: 'Above all others, men of genius and learning shared the principal place in his favour; and in these he had much discernment: for though he had missed the advantage of a learned education, yet being blest with vast natural abilities, he had so well profited by a vigorous, though late application to Letters, and by much conversation with men of eminence in this way, that he was himself a very competent judge in most kinds of literature'. Allen to a T, one might think

There is more along these lines, indeed to the point where some critics found the character of Squire Allworthy a bit too good to be true. Fielding had several quite venomous detractors.

Another visitor to Prior Park that summer was a young friend of William Warburton's, Charles Yorke, who wrote a spontaneous tribute to Ralph Allen:

Letter from Charles Yorke to the Rev William Warburton
September 1746

Sir

Tho I was most naturally disappointed not to find you at Prior Park, the loss of your company was quite made up for by the great kindness and politeness with which I was received by the owners themselves of Prior Park. The natural beauties of wood, water, prospect, hill and vale, wildness and cultivation, make it one of the most delightful spots I ever saw, without adding anything from art. The elegance and judgment with which art has been employed, and the affectation of false grandeur carefully avoided, make one wonder how it could be so busy there, without spoiling any thing received from nature. But even scenes of this kind, which had alone made other places agreeable in my journey, were the least of its charms to me. I soon found those scenes animated by the presence of the master: the tranquillity and harmony of the whole only reflecting back the image of his own temper: an appearance of wealth and plenty with plainness and frugality; and yet no one envying, because all are warmed into friendship and gratitude by the rays of his benevolence.

Yours etc
Charles Yorke

DIARY
February 23 1747

Today the fifth contract for the cross-road and bye-way letters has been approved by the Lords of the Treasury. The Postmasters General, the Earl of Leicester and Sir Everard Fawkener, recommended that my petition for the seven year extension should be granted. I have now offered to supply at my own cost a six-day post between London and Taunton, Exeter and Bristol, and also between London and Worcester and Birmingham via Oxford. I will speed up the cross-road posts between Exeter, Bristol and Birmingham, and on the western road to Dorchester and Weymouth, and I have guaranteed a £500 increase in the produce of country letters. Their Lordships have also approved a continuing annual payment by myself of £6,000.

September 12 1747

I have been spending much time on my project to make the Avon navigable to Melksham, a dozen miles east of Bath. It will benefit both the commerce of this part of the county, and secure a permanent income for the Bath Hospital. It requires a petition to Parliament for the scheme, and I have been busy working on a draft.

We have had great pleasure in Mr Fielding's company here this summer. He has such experiences in the London and literary and theatrical world that one never tires of his conversation, yet he is as interested in our life here, our friends and our family, as in anyone in that City. Of course he has extensive knowledge of the law and of those who break it – yet I think he has a mind so generous that he does not judge, nor even condemn, anyone. I sometimes feel I have seen little compared to him, but perhaps I have learned much from the world of stone, from the masons, the engineers, the men who build and design and create the world we live in, and whom perhaps those who live solely in the world of letters are inclined to take for granted.

Nevertheless Ralph Allen was very much a 'man of Letters', although not a great hand at writing them himself. But he had always loved books. His library in the Long Gallery at Prior Park was filling with new volumes, among them an edition of Shakespeare edited by William Warburton and dedicated to Mrs Allen - in whom, he said, he had found modesty, devotion to her husband's happiness, and also 'friendship, generosity, and the benevolence of charity, added to every female virtue that most adorns your sex'. Fortunately she probably didn't study the edition too closely –Warburton had 'improved' Shakespeare to the point of ridicule even from contemporary critics. But there were novels, too, like Samuel Richardson's new book *Clarissa*, and a wonderful copy of Admiral George Anson's *Voyage Round The World in 1740*, which Allen had bound and gilded for his library. This was a grand time for literature. Swift, Johnson, Fielding and Richardson, Joseph Addison and Richard Steele, Tobias Smollett and Laurence Sterne, and many other writers, philosophers and poets, added a new richness to the age. Ralph Allen was an eager enthusiast and patron.

9.

Crowds came to marvel at Ralph Allen's railway carrying stone
from Combe Down to his wharf on the River Avon at Widcombe.
The road called Ralph Allen's Drive follows the line of the railway.

10.
John Wood designed the perfect vernacular architecture of Allen's Combe Down terrace of houses for his quarrymen. This one, Dial House in Church Road, was the home of Allen's Clerk of Works, Richard Jones.

11.
Alexander Pope, friend of Allen, was short in stature and somewhat deformed, and the Allens provided a special green velvet chair to make him comfortable.

12.

Gertrude, 'Little Gatty', Allen's niece, married the Rev William Warburton who was much older than her. She was to inherit Prior Park after the death of her mother.

13.
James Wolfe, hero of Quebec, once lived at this house in Trim Street, built in 1720, with symbols of his military triumph over the doorway.

14.
Widcombe Manor was the home of the Bennett family, and Allen's nephew Philip married Jane Bennett.

15.
'Little Gatty', Allen's niece, heard Alexander Pope's lady friend in his room at Prior Park *very* early in the morning – and passed this nugget on to feed the gossip...

16.
The Bath Mineral Water Hospital, now the Royal National
Hospital for Rheumatic Diseases - without its later storey.

17.
Ralph Allen took the Cornish chough as his personal emblem.
Once extinct in Cornwall, it is now breeding there again.

DIARY
March 26 1748

General Wade died ten days past. He was 75, so
it was a good age, but it has greatly saddened me.
He was perhaps the first to believe in me, the first
to offer patronage – but not only patronage, indeed,
friendship over all these years, for we have had
much in common, despite the differences in our
lives. He too was of no wealthy family, and joined
the army in Westmeath in Ireland at the age of
17, just as I came here to Bath at that same age.
We both took a hand in shaping our own lives. He
will be sorely missed by many, for he has been a
servant of four Kings, a patron and benefactor of
many. His estate was considerable and I believe
will go to his natural sons, with a bequest to Mrs
Erle, his natural daughter. He has left £100 to me
and another £100 to Mr Van Diest, the painter,
who I know is in need of such good fortune, for he
has not been well. I have done what I can to help
him but I fear his suffering is too great.

May 13 1748

It seems that the war has come to an end, at least
there are rumours of it: I have made it my business
to find out if freight costs for stone shipped to
London from Bristol may be lower than during
hostilities. I suspect not, for no one can say if this
cessation of arms is temporary or not. I shall write
to the Governors of St Bartholomew's Hospital to
let them know I will resume sending and working
stone for them as soon as I can secure a vessel.

The War of the Austrian Succession came to a formal end early in 1749. Like so many such conflicts, it had not directly affected those countries involved in it, but shipping routes had been disrupted and made even more dangerous. The proclamation of the peace was celebrated in Bath, as in many towns across the country, with bell ringing and bonfires.

DIARY
February 12 1749

I have written to the Governors of St Bartholomew's that there don't appear to me the least probability of being able to finish the building of the new wing this year. Nor do I believe that even if it was practicable, it would be prudent to attempt the covering of so large and high a building as that is, in one year. Only one or two storeys should be erected, and the stone allowed to settle and harden before the third is added.

Mr Wood has shown me his second edition of his 'Essay towards a Description of Bath.' Whereas in the first he made no mention of me, there is now much on the subject of my work, with several large folding pictures of Prior Park. And Mr Anthony Walker is come to work upon his perspective drawings of the estate, which will be of great interest to all, not only to myself.

DIARY
May 14 1750

Bath has never been so full of the frivolous, the fashionable and the false…Not a few days ago there were upwards of seven hundred people at the ball at Simpson's Great Room, and Mr Nash has introduced the game of EO from Tunbridge Wells – it is a kind of Even or Odds, hence the name, and played with a ball and a kind of revolving gallery into which the ball may fall at a certain point. Here we have had the Rev John Brown, another protégé of Mr Warburton, staying on after both were here for a while. Mr Brown has preached in the Abbey on the evils of false happiness, especially that of gambling. He is, of course, right in his views, yet I cannot always be so severe as he is…

Letter from Ralph Allen to Charles Yorke
August 2 1750

Sir

We have had the singular honour of a visit from the Prince of Wales, here at Prior Park. I would that you would not gossip, but I found it somewhat disconcerting to find that although the Prince seemed quick in apprehending, and interested, he soon appeared to know nothing.

Yours etc
Ralph Allen

A visit from the Prince of Wales sealed Ralph Allen's reputation. He was now well established in polite society, as well as the ever more influential world of business and trade. There were increasing numbers of visitors to Prior Park, including not only writers but actors and musicians, among them David Garrick, James Quin, and Handel.

DIARY
October 17 1750

We have had a most delightful and bracing visit to Weymouth, returning just this last sen'night. It is the most sweet, clean, agreeable town, the sea air and splendid long beach doing us all a great deal of good. Elizabeth is much refreshed. My Cold Bath at Prior Park is excellent and most efficacious, but cannot in truth compare with bathing in the cool sea water at Weymouth. Also the drinking of sea water is being recommended by a number of physicians. We have decided that we shall build a house for us all on the harbour, not a great house but something suitable for a month or so in the summer. We will be only some 65 miles distant from Bath, and I can continue most of my business from there.

They now have some of the new bathing machines in Weymouth – little bath houses on wheels, with two clean napkins and a servant, drawn by a horse out to the required depth, after which it is left there and the servant and the horse return until the bather signals to be returned to the shore.

It is so very restful to be beside the sea again. It makes me think of my childhood in Cornwall, when we were not so far from the sea as we are now in Bath. I have decided to make the Cornish chough my emblem, for it is the native bird of Cornwall, and indeed a charming, mischievous, amusing creature.

Ralph Allen can take some credit for making Weymouth fashionable, although the sea air and salt water were already, as he says, being recommended by physicians. Tradition has it that he built a house at 2 Trinity Road, backing on to the harbour. He was very fond of the town and entertained, among others, the brother of King George II, the young Duke of York, when he was with the Royal Naval fleet sheltering in Weymouth Bay. Other families followed the Allens. Almost 40 years later, in 1789, George III visited the town. He liked it so much that he bought a house there, and established Weymouth as a leading seaside resort.

DIARY
August 28 1751

We are in Weymouth once more, and hope that the sea air will help to aid Elizabeth's recovery, for she has been so extremely ill since May that we have feared for her life.   Bathing in salt water seems to help her, though she remains very infirm of body.

After our departure I was sent news of the death of a mason working in one of the quarries at Claverton Down when the stone fell in upon him. I have written to his widow and promised she will receive financial help for her and her family.   It grieves me so much when there are accidents of this kind, one is forever wondering what might have been in place to prevent it.

I have had two silver sauce boats engraved with a Cornish chough, as a small present to cheer Elizabeth as she returns to health.

Mr Fielding tells me that he is hoping for publication of his new novel, 'Amelia', to take place before Christmas.   He has written to me in most generous terms asking if it might be dedicated to me.

The new year, 1752, started with some problems: a certain Shaderick Cooper stole several of the fir trees Allen had planted at Bathampton – he planted some 55,000 trees on his total estate. He offered a reward of £10, and the thief was swiftly captured. And there were family difficulties. Gertrude Tucker, now married to William Warburton, was concerned about her brother William (Billy) who was now in the Royal Navy. He had been posted to Jamaica as a lieutenant but the post was not one he wanted. Gertrude must have had some sort of argument, possibly about Billy, with her aunt, Mrs Allen, because later Ralph was constrained to write to placate her:

Letter from Ralph Allen to Gertrude Warburton
February 1752

My Dear Child

In answer to the letter which I this morning received from you, I have the Satisfaction to acquaint you that you are much mistaken in the coolness which you apprended from your Aunt, and I am sure your return will be very agreeable to her, and from me brighten your own conceptions of the tenderness that you will certainly receive from me.

I am concern'd after all the pains which I have taken for Billy's going abroad on the best terms which the greatest of my Interests can obtain for him to hear of any foolish dislike from himself. I last night tho much out of order just desired Mr Warburton to acquaint him how absolutely necessary his going is.

I've lately by the bad weather and too much business had my slowness of breath and a disagreeable heaviness strong upon me, but I am better than I was yesterday. My kindest wishes attend you all and I am beyond Expressions.

Yours most affectionately
R Allen

More trouble that year: the issue of Dr Cleland, who had been dismissed by the committee of the Governors of the Bath Hospital following allegations of assault of two women, was raised once more by the author of a pamphlet. The author happened to be Tobias Smollett, a novelist of repute, and also, as it happened, a surgeon. He was intent on justice for Cleland, as he saw it, and his description of Bath and the baths in particular is coruscating. He describes them vividly in *The Adventures of Humphrey Clinker,* published after his death.

"Two days ago I went into the King's Bath, in order to clear the strainer of the skin, for the benefit of a free perspiration; and the first object that saluted my eye was a child full of scrofulus ulcers, carried in the arms of one of the guides, under the very noses of the bathers. I was so shocked at the sight, that I retired immediately with indignation and disgust – suppose that the matter of those ulcers, floating on the water, comes in contact with my skin, when the pores are all open, I would ask you what must be the consequence? Good Heaven, the very thought makes my blood run cold! We know not what sores may be running into the water while we are bathing, and what sort of matter we may thus imbibe... But I am now as much afraid of drinking, as of bathing; for after a long conversation with the Doctor, about the construction of the pump and the cistern, it is very far from being clear with me, that the patients in the Pump Room don't swallow the scourings of the bathers."

Smollett, in the person of the extremely grumpy Matthew Bramble, continues in this vein for a considerable time:

"In order to avoid this filthy composition, I had recourse to the spring that supplies the private baths on the Abbey Green; but I at once perceived something extraordinary in the taste and smell; and, upon inquiry, I find that the Roman baths in this quarter, were found covered by an old burying ground, belonging to the Abbey; through which, in all probability, the water drains in its passage so that as we drink the decoction of living bodies at the Pump Room, we swallow the strainings of rotten bones and carcasses at the private bath – I vow to God, the very idea turns my stomach!"

Fortunately Mr Bramble's niece, Lydia, has a more favourable view of the City:

"Bath is to me a new world – all is gaiety, good humour, and diversion. At eight in the morning, we go in dishabille to the Pump

Room, which is crowded like a Welsh fair; and there you see the highest quality, and the lowest trades folks, jostling each other, without ceremony, hail-fellow well-met. The noise of the music playing in the gallery, the heat and flavour of such a crowd, and hum and buzz of their conversation, gave me the headache and vertigo the first day; but afterwards, all these things became familiar, and even agreeable. Right under the Pump Room windows is the King's Bath; a huge cistern, where you see the patients up to their necks in hot water. The ladies wear jackets and petticoats of brown linen, with chip hats, in which they fix their handkerchiefs to wipe the sweat from their faces; but, truly, whether it is owing to the steam that surrounds them, or the heat of the water, or the nature of the dress, or to all these causes together, they look so flushed, and so frightful, that I always turn my eyes another way – for my part, I content myself with drinking about half a pint of the water every morning. It is the only hot water I could ever drink, without being sick – Far from having that effect, it is rather agreeable to the taste, grateful to the stomach, and reviving to the spirits. You cannot imagine what wonderful cures it performs – my uncle began with it the other day; but he made wry faces in drinking, and I'm afraid he will leave it off."

It is possible that Ralph Allen met Smollett, but they were certainly not likely to become friends.

DIARY
September 28 1752

It has been quite a summer: we learned in July that Princess Amelia, wife of the Duke of Cumberland, was suffering from a nervous complaint that greatly affected her hearing, and that she had decided to come to her favourite spa for a cure. But she also let it be known that she wished to stay at Prior Park, and we had no choice therefore, this being something of a royal command, but to vacate Prior Park (as indeed we intended to, so it was no real hardship) and allow her to take possession for some three or four weeks in August. She apparently arrived late in the afternoon of the seventh of August, with a large retinue, and was met with bell ringing and cannon fire. She stayed at Prior Park only ten days before moving down into the town, since each day she attended the Pump Room between seven and eight o'clock for her first glass of water…

And of course we have lost eleven days this summer – Parliament has decreed that England should be brought up to date with the rest of Europe and move from the old Julian calendar to the Gregorian. It appears that for centuries the Julian calendar had permitted each year to last eleven minutes longer than it had a physical right so to do. On September 2, therefore, the whole nation went to bed and woke up on September 14.

We missed the fifty-mile horse race on Claverton Down, it being in August, but indeed Weymouth has amusement enough for us all.

In 1754, just after the foundation stone for The Circus was laid in February of that year, John Wood died. He was 50. His son had been his assistant for some years past, and now, at 26, took on the mantle of his father's vision, sharing both his ideas and his talent. Many believe that John Wood the Elder deserves to be better known beyond the City of Bath: he did much to change the whole aesthetic of the way people regarded cities and the planning of our towns today. At the time of his death he had undoubtedly changed Bath forever. Although his dream of redesigning it as a splendid Roman city expressing the magical qualities of an ancient Druidic civilization was never realized, through his own and his son's work it came very close.

The Woods were not the only architects of Bath, but they have left the most unified and imaginative legacy. By the time he died, John Wood the Elder had seen Queen Square completed, with its unique palatial composition, and had laid the foundation stone for The Circus. Chapel Court at St John's Hospital and part of Gay Street (finished by his son to link Queen Square with The Circus, as his father had planned) were also complete.

John Wood had transformed the muddy riversides along the Avon by building the great Parades, North and South, with Duke Street and Pierrepont Street, some five metres above the river, constructed on stone vaults to form wide paved terraces. These became airy promenades for the fashionable to stroll in the sunshine and look across at the meadows of Bathwick. It was a part of his vision of a great Roman Forum. Here too was Terrace Walk, with its shops and coffee houses, close to Ralph Alien's town house. Nearby were Mr Harrison's Lower Assembly Rooms, focus of society. The Orange Grove, given its name after the Prince of Orange came to take the waters in 1734, was a place to saunter on the gravel walks and admire the flowers. Not far away was the new Theatre Royal (built by another architect, Thomas Jelly - for by now there were many in Bath) and Wood's charming little backwater of Pierrepont Place. Just beyond the Orange Grove were the Abbey, the Baths and the Pump Room. A short walk away was the Bath General Hospital, joint venture of Beau Nash, John Wood and Ralph Allen. To the south, high in its deep wooded combe, was Prior Park.

John Wood died just 15 months before the discovery which would have seemed to him like another confirmation of his vision of ancient Bath. Close to the Abbey were found the remains of a Saxon cemetery, and then what appeared to be Roman remains, now known to be the east end of the Roman baths complex.

DIARY
May 30 1754

It is hard to believe that John Wood is no longer with us. He was not so much younger than me. He was fifty, only nine years younger, when he died three days ago here in Bath. We met when we were both young men, and full of zest for life, he with his Grand Plan for the City, I perhaps more earthbound, more mundane, perhaps, with my own ideas for business and expansion of the posts and the quarries. Yet we were linked from the beginning, for not only did we share a vision of the City through the Stone, but perhaps shared a sense always of being in some way on the outside of society, for my part because I had no inheritance of wealth or privilege, and on his because he was forever on the edge of some financial crisis or other. I do not think he has ever been given recognition sufficient for his talent. His interests in antiquities such as Stonehenge and the ancient legends sometimes distracted him from his architectural work, and he had a way of – well, shall I say, he was somewhat lacking in urbanity and charm when it came to persuading those who had the means to offer him patronage.

I remember, when we first met, and he was working on the rebuilding of St John's Hospital for the Duke of Chandos (owner of the great mansion, Cannons, in London), he was full of a wonderful Palladian scheme for Bath. Indeed, the buildings for St John's Hospital were to be a part of it, and from the beginning the facades were so new and classical that much comment was heard. Unfortunately the interiors were not of so excellent a construction, and he and Chandos were at odds for a deal of time after it – although in truth I think the old man and the young free spirit understood each other well enough. As, indeed, did Mr Wood and myself: we had hot words over the work on my house in the City, and more when he began the plans for Prior Park, but never fell out for long, and I would have had no other with me on such projects – the Bristol Exchange is one of which I think we both felt exceedingly proud.

I do believe John Wood did much to change the very shape of cities: his airy atria, squares and pavilions, his vision of Bath as a kind of Palladian jewel set among hills which themselves are set with villas of comparable beauty, are unique to him. He saw a town, a city, as a whole, not as individual buildings. And he loved the Stone. For us both, it was the Stone that we set out to make manifest to the world. I wish he had had more time to fulfil his ambitions. Yet at least he has a son. The younger John has already been working upon the plans for the Circus with his father, and I doubt not they will reach fruition. I always envied him his son...

I shall miss him. More, perhaps, than I foresaw. He and I were united in our belief in this City, in our vision for its future. We made mistakes, we were distracted, but no matter, in the end we had a bond unlike any other. I would that in time he will be known for his gifts as an architect to match any other of his time.

October 12 1754

I have had word that Henry Fielding has died in Portugal. It has come as no great surprise, for he has been ill enough in all conscience in these past few years, not just with the gout and asthma but other afflictions – he was on crutches when last we met. I am to be executor of his Will, a task I shall carry out with the greatest diligence, for so humane and compassionate a man I never saw equalled. He was a great writer but perhaps an even greater force for justice as London's Chief Magistrate and in all his writings. I braver man I never met. His wife and children will be my care always.

We have had many guests at Prior Park in recent weeks, among them Mr Thomas Potter, who is – or in any case undoubtedly considers himself to be – a person of unequalled wit and charm. Well, so it may be, but I have had some concerns about his familiarity with Gertrude, since her husband is currently in London... Mr Potter is a friend of William Pitt, for whom indeed I have the greatest respect and, I trust, a friendship of some little time past, but he has exercised his wit and charm on Gertrude with what appears to be considerable success. I have tried to remark upon it to her, but she only laughs at me, and takes no notice of any chiding...

Thomas Potter, son of the Archbishop of Canterbury, was a notorious rake, a member of the infamous 'Monks of Medenham' club led by Sir Francis Dashwood – otherwise known as the Hellfire Club, where a lot of drinking, wenching and general blasphemy was enjoyed by wealthy and not so wealthy young men.   Potter and his confidant John Wilkes wrote a lewd parody of Alexander Pope's great work *An Essay on Man*, calling it *An Essay on Woman*.

Nevertheless Thomas Potter became a regular visitor at Prior Park, and must have had a good deal of charm.   That October, he wrote to John Wilkes that 'the Pedant' – his name for Gertrude Warburton's husband William –had departed from Prior Park, and that he himself intended to seduce Mrs Warburton during his absence. Gertrude evidently had charm of her own. She made friends easily, men and women: her doctor in Weymouth described her as 'elegant in her person, possessed of an excellent understanding, great politeness, and a most engaging naivete in conversation'. Quite what, if any, relationship there might have been is not recorded.

DIARY
July 27 1755

Three deaths this year in the quarries at Combe Down and Odd Down, for all that I have tried to make them safer by altering the entrances. I have done what I can for the families.

I feel some anxiety about young Billy (William Tucker) who has done so well in his profession in the Royal Navy, yet despite the country being on the eve of a naval war is without a promotion nor command in sight. I have applied to Mr Yorke (Charles Yorke, whom Allen first encountered when he was a young friend of William Warburton's, and who was now MP and brother-in-law of Admiral George Anson, having recently been married) but have received no reply. Gertrude has written with her usual frankness, so I am hoping for some response.

Letter from Gertrude Warburton to Charles Yorke, MP

July 17
Sir

My Brother has served in the Navy long enough to see many of his Juniors preferred to the command of Ships. His conduct has been such as his Friends have no reason to blush at, and he is now, at the recommendation of my Uncle's friend Sir John Ligonier, third Lieutenant of the Ship in which Admiral Holbourne has hoisted his Flag. Your connexion with Lord Anson gives you the power of serving my Brother. He wishes to have the command of a Sloop, or Tender, in order to his being preferr'd, in turn, to the command Ship, and this I am sure you may procure for him.

Yours affectionately
Gertrude Warburton

No reply came: Gertrude wrote again, reproachfully:

When you was a Batchelor you was not so inattentive, and I have a better opinion of matrimony, than to suppose it can have worked so ill a change.

She did get a reply in the end, although Charles Yorke was distinctly embarrassed over the requests. Billy got his command in the following July.

DIARY
October 22
1755

A quiet year so far, at least, though abroad there is the threat of War, and I have discussed this a good deal with Mr Pitt, (William Pitt the Elder) who since his marriage to Lady Hester Grenville has been much restored in confidence and energy. He has apparently discovered the delights of gardening – he is much taken with my new flowery meadow-lawn in the orchard, and is urging me to build a Gothick ruin of some kind upon the hill at Hampton Down, so that it may be viewed by visitors from the Terrace Walk and the Parades to charm all visitors to Bath. It seems that such Gothick adornments are all the rage...

Ralph Allen did build his 'Sham Castle' – or, at least, his Clerk of Works Richard Jones built it – but not until seven years later.   It is still visible from the Parades today.

William Pitt was already a formidable figure in British politics, charismatic, a great orator and a man of irreproachable, if sometimes arrogant, character.   He was implacably resolute in pursuing the Seven Years' War with France, which began in 1756. It was the first essentially global war, encompassing India and North America as well as Europe. The spark was Austria's attempt to win back the province of Silesia from Prussia, and then France's capture of the Mediterranean island of Menorca from Britain. Britan, led by Pitt, finally triumphed, becoming the dominant colonial and maritime power.   Pitt resigned as Secretary of State in 1757 but was recalled by popular demand, and went on to success with his vigorous war policy. He resigned again, this time for good, in 1761, when the majority of the cabinet refused to declare war on Spain.

Ralph Allen liked William Pitt, and he was a frequent visitor at Prior Park – much to the irritation of William Warburton, who did not like him at all.   By now Pitt had a house in Bath, and a year later would become MP for the City, with considerable help from Allen.

Another visitor at Prior Park was the actor, theatre manager and playwright, David Garrick, who became a tenant of the Allens' house at Bathhampton. And despite the declaration of War on May 18 there was a lot of happiness at Prior Park that year.

DIARY
May 19 1756

Such juxtaposition – yesterday, a Declaration of War: a few days earlier, the birth of a son to Gatty and William [Warburton]. He was christened Ralph at Widcombe Church only two days ago. It is a wonderful thing to me that I should have this little man here – it is like to having a grandson, as if little George was in some way come back to us.

Gertrude was 29 then, her husband William Warburton 58. There was talk, probably then, certainly later, that the father of Gertrude's child was in fact Thomas Potter, who had boasted to John Wilkes about seducing her. But it seems from the correspondence between Potter and others that this was probably not true. At this time Potter wrote to Pitt:

The scenes at Prior Park change every hour; but the worthy owner has a heart that cannot change. The present joy at the birth of an heir does not respite the labours of the gardener. Half the summer will show the bridge; the dairy opens to the lake; vast woods have taken possession of the naked hills; and the lawns slope uninterrupted to the valleys.

DIARY
October 2 1756

Good and bad things this year. First, the good: we have achieved much at Prior Park, with the new dairy building for Beauty, Daisy, Brown, Blossom and Violet and their sisters – there is something most satisfying about the sight of cows grazing in the valley. Little Ralph, of course: and then the new bridge. It is quite perfect. Richard Jones used the plans of its model at Lord Pembroke's Wilton House, which he had built for the grounds there some twenty years ago – indeed I believe there are other copies. Yet it is so exquisitely elegant, so delicate, that it cannot be bettered. It spans just that part of the ponds in the valley so as to draw the eye, to add just that touch of Man's art that so perfectly complements Nature.

Also I have been much tried by the Governors of St Bartholomew's Hospital, demanding more stone for a fourth wing of the Hospital – I wrote last month to say that I hadn't the least rational expectation of being able to send any Stone from Bristol to London during the present War. What irks me in particular is that when they had almost completed the third wing of the Hospital, I had sent them an overplus of stone in order that they might begin the fourth wing: they it was who told me to dispose of the stone, which I did at a considerable loss. I have told them I will do what I can, but I suspect – and hope – that they may have the wit to postpone the building.

However even less pleasing is the publication of 'Essay on Waters' by the Irish apothecary (and, I would hazard, failed Irish politician) Charles Lucas, who calls himself a 'political knight errant', and on the strength of a medical degree from the Netherlands considers himself to be 'in quest of physical truths, not private gain'. However he has taken it upon himself to devote one hundred and twenty pages of his work to attack this City, its physicians, its Aldermen and, most devastating of all, its Waters. He accuses the doctors of 'Sloth, Indolence or Ignorance', and the water of having almost no value for any sickness or condition whatever. He persuades his readers that the water is neither saponaceous nor sulphureous, nitrous nor alkaline; that the green colour of the Baths is just algae; and that the water contains only a little iron, a little marine salt, a little lime! Dr (Samuel) Johnson has reviewed the work, and that has given it no little publicity in London, where I believe Mr Lucas has set up as some sort of physician himself. Were it not for the attacks on Dr Oliver and others, I must add that some of his writing on the City is of interest, for he describes the newly uncovered Roman remains, the new architecture and the fact that Bath stone is similar to that of Paris.

Charles Lucas had only just escaped imprisonment in Newgate when he caused some trouble in Ireland by his views on the British rule there, and fled to London. His investigation of the spa waters of Europe included those of Belgium and Germany. Later he would return to Ireland and continue to harass the establishment, often with good reason. Quite what response he got from the City of Bath is not recorded, but there was a lot of truth in his analysis of the Hot Spring Waters. His conclusion basically was that any complaint might be aided by the drinking of warm water with a few minerals and some salt... Nevertheless, the Bath Hot Spring Water is special. You only have to look at the most recent investigation.

The water that pours out of the Hot Springs in Bath flows at the rate of 1.3 million litres a day at an average temperature of 45 degrees Centigrade. It fell to the earth some 10,000 years ago and must have descended up to 3 kilometres to reach its current stable temperature on returning to the surface. It contains 42 minerals and trace elements including calcium, sulphate, bicarbonate and sodium – and a small amount of iron.

The newly uncovered Roman remains, to which Allen refers, were just south of the Abbey, and had been revealed during a new suite of baths called the Duke of Kingston Baths.

But the affair of the Bath waters was not over: Charles Lucas continued his attack, specifically on Dr William Oliver, and the following year Dr William Baylies added his own rubbishing of the waters in his book *Practical Reflections on the Uses and Abuses of Bath Waters, Made from Actual Experiments and Observations...* Dr Oliver was robust in his defence:

Letter from Dr William Oliver to Ralph Allen
August 6 1757

Dear Allen

I am putting together case histories of fifteen of
my patients (sufferers from Leprosy, Scurvy,
Rheumatism and so on) in order to publish a proper
analysis of the efficacious nature of the Bath water.
In any case I detect some unpleasant resentfulness
in these attacks, so aimed at myself as they are. I
suspect it may be that there is some envy here: I
know Dr Lucas suffers horridly from the gout, and
I myself am indeed well even at the age of sixty-
three: I have my family, my friends, my paintings
and books, and perhaps most important of all from
their point of view I do unconscionably well from
the dispensing of my Oliver Biscuits...

Yours etc
Dr William Oliver

Bath Oliver Biscuits are still a best-seller, now throughout
the world. Some say that Dr Oliver also invented the Bath
Bun, with its delicious lump of melted sugar inside and
sugar crystals on its shiny surface, and that it was because
his patients were getting so fat on Bath Buns that he thought
of an antidote in the thin dry Bath Oliver biscuit. Legend
has it that the biscuits were baked by Dr Oliver's coachman,
to whom, late in life, Dr Oliver gave the recipe, together
with a hundred pounds and some bags of fine white flour.
The story was handed down through members of the Oliver
family, although the subsequent manufacturers, Fortt

and Son of Bath, had no information about the source
of the recipe because their factory was bombed in 1941.
Bath Olivers are now made in Liverpool for the French
multinational Groupe Danone.

DIARY
July 10 1757

Yesterday a triumph here in the City, though
perhaps the real victor was absent – Mr Pitt,
Our 'Great Commoner', is now elected Member of
Parliament for Bath. Thomas Potter represented
him. I myself worked with Mr Pitt on the contents
of his letter of acceptance, read out by Mr Potter.
There has had to be a certain amount of difficulty
in negotiating the shifts of parliamentary seats
between here in Bath, Okehampton and Aylesbury,
thus allowing Mr Pitt to move from Okehampton
to here, but all has been agreed, and I do believe
that Mr Pitt is the right man to pursue the Whig
doctrine of foreign trade and colonial expansion,
even at the cost of war. Mr Pitt has written to me
most geneous and indeed affectionate thanks.

Letter from Ralph Allen to William Pitt
July 12 1757

I am most appreciative of your thanks, Dear Sir, and for me the Satisfaction is in having everything in Bath just as you wished it, which makes me very happy; as does also the sense that I have faithfully discharged my duty to my country in the affair.

I am, Dear Sir, Your most honoured and most obedient Servant,
Ralph Allen

That year, Pitt's energetic policy saw the tide of the War turning in Britain's favour.

DIARY
September 2
1757

The painter Mr Arthur Pond has painted a portrait of myself, in the study at Prior Park. I am not sure that it does me justice. I look a little old.

DIARY
March 22 1758

After much negotiation I have now acquired Claverton Manor, with its thirteen hundred acres of high downs, hillsides, and a valley of the Avon. It is most beautiful, set as it is down in the valley, with the woods and hills to the east, and the house itself a most elegant and charming Jacobean mansion with many barns and an ancient church close by. I now have in my care two little churches, tho' this at Claverton has in its accounts a grand total of less than five pounds, and the greatest problem has been in getting rid of twelve foxes, nine polecats and two hundred and thirty sparrows. The annual dinner for the rector cost two shillings and sixpence.

I can now ride from Prior Park up to Combe Down, then across the level hill top with its views to the south and east of such unparalleled beauty that I could live nowhere else but here – then a steep descent to Claverton and my new house. It would not please Mr Wood, I am sure, for it is full of strapwork, carved overmantels, oriel windows and gables, so that the whole has a kind of romantic atmosphere that I have to admit to myself is something cosier, pehaps, than the sparer elegance of Prior Park. I have commissioned the drawing of a great survey of the Manors of Hampton, Claverton and Widcombe, to include all my properties and bridges and summerhouses, and the Cornish chough as emblem.

I note, however, that Claverton Down is the setting for some unfortunate behaviour these days, including duels and highway robberies and all kinds of folly. I would not deny the crowds the pleasures of the race course, but I am minded to warn that such accompanying misbehaviour will not now be tolerated by the new owner...

The warning duly appeared in *The Bath Journal* of September 4th that year:

> "Whereas Ralph Allen, Esq, hath permitted his Down to be used for the next Races, it is to be presumed no Person will think himself treated with severity if he has an Action brought against him for doing any Damage to the Plantations on the Down, or the Walls thereof. A Watch will be set at each Plantation; and after this Notice, every Person who shall trespass will be deemed wilful Trespassers, and prosecuted as such.
> If any Person hath a Dog, that he wants to be shot or hanged, if he will produce him on the Down his Wish shall be gratify'd, Persons being hired for that Purpose from this time 'till the Races are over."

A week later the Journal listed two horses owned by William Pitt as running at Claverton, 'Mr Pitt's horse Tickler, alias Old England, and his bay horse Liberty' – both won in the same week. 'What could be more cheering to Bath, to Ralph Allen, and the free citizens of the nation?'

The last recorded horse race at Claverton was in 1796, after which Bath Races moved to Lansdown on the north side of the City.

DIARY
September 18
1758

Weymouth is good for us all this year. I have had more trials with the Governors of St Bartholomew's Hospital, urgently requiring more freestone for the fourth wing; I have had to write repeating all I said last year about the problems of shipping in wartime. I have told them that the freight rates would be more than I could bear. I offered to take all the unused Bath stone off their hands, plus donating £500 to the Hospital, but they are adamant. There are times – many times, if I am honest – that I wish I had repudiated the contract, which after all was made so long ago, indeed 28 years, under such different circumstances. I would of course be greatly pleased to see the Hospital complete with its fourth wing of the quadrangle, but I had never anticipated that it would be at such cost to me.

However wartime made Weymouth the more stimulating for us, because the fleet was kept in Weymouth Bay during gales in the Channel. It was commanded by Commodore Howe under the Duke of York, and the house was constantly full with a great many of their officers. And little Ralph, now two and some months, was a continuing delight – he has even drawn a picture of me.

DIARY
August 4 1759

I have had a most agonising attack of the Gravel. Kind messages have been sent to us here at Prior Park and I am recovering. And there has been sad news. Word has come of the death of Mr Thomas Potter, who only a year ago entertained us all in Bath with a dinner and a ball for the Corporation, celebrating his new position as Recorder of the City. Many spoke ill of him but he was a stout supporter of Mr Pitt's policy towards the War. William [Warburton] tells me that Gertrude says that poor Potter's death has made her a moralist, that she now sees the vanity of all worldly pursuits and has seen a man "sacrificing his quiet, his health, and his fortune, to his ambition, who in the forty-first year of his age died unpossessed of every comfort of a rational being". I always thought Gertrude had a particular fondness for Mr Potter... There is another death, too, perhaps in its way a sadder one: Charles Yorke's wife, whom he married only four years ago, has recently died. She was only young. I have managed to write to him, for I know only too well what sorrow it is to lose someone.

'The Gravel' probably meant kidney stones – undoubtedly very painful.

Letter from Ralph Allen to Charles Yorke MP
August 4 1759

My Dear Charles

A severe illness hindered me from sooner sending to you my sincerest condolence for your exceeding great loss, but now I beg leave to do it in the heartiest manner. I sensibly felt it from the moment I heard it and pray God to soften your grief and support you under one of the most trying afflictions that can attend a good and tender mind.

Your devoted friend,
Ralph Allen

DIARY
December 22 1759

Much excitement as the war against the French goes so well, particularly in the Americas. I have put up Mr Henry Popple's map of North America so that we may follow the campaign, for it clearly shows the English, French and Spanish colonial possessions. Billy is taking part in the naval actions. And of course we have the wonderful capture of Quebec by General James Wolfe, although our rejoicing was much tempered by news of his death. I arranged for candles to be lit everywhere in Prior Park, at every window visible to the city below, in his honour. The Bath Advertiser said the house "in Splendour outshone anything in imagination, being one grand Appearance of Light, and gave a very fine idea of the Chinese Feast of Lanterns, which with a large Bonfire a little on its right, made the most sparkling and lively Appearance ever yet seen."

Indeed, so many French prisoners are there that the Government has made a haven for them at Bideford in Devon. I have organised a subscription to provide them with warm clothing and other assistance, with money being paid in at Mr Leake's bookshop and Mr Morgan's Coffee House.

Almost more excitement at the news that William [Warburton] has finally been given a bishopric. It is Gloucester, and due much to the kind assistance of Mr Pitt. The Bath Advertiser has today described him as 'that masterly Writer, uncommon Genius, and Prodigy of Learning, the judicious Dr Warburton, to the See of Gloucester, thus filling the hearts of the studious and learned Clergy with Joy and Gladness'. A little too fulsome, perhaps. Of course William is now sixty-two: Gertrude, however, a deal younger. I believe she will enjoy her new role. William is to be consecrated at Lambeth on January 20th.

My portrait (by Mr William Hoare) has been presented to the Governors of the Exeter Hospital. I am pleased with it.

The *Bath Advertiser* was first published in October 1755. In 1760 it became the *Bath Chronicle*, today Bath's weekly local newspaper.

DIARY
June 8 1760

Poor Beau Nash is in a bad way. He is now 86 years old, and although it is true that his reduced circumstances are in no small way due to his own extravagance, ruinous appetites and vanity, nevertheless he has done so much for this City that one cannot but pity him. He has announced that he is to write his autobiography, and has asked for subscriptions to the venture – the Bath Council voted in February to give him ten guineas every month towards it. Many who once were his most unctuous supplicants now dismiss him entirely. However I have been as ready as I can be to help the old showman – for such he was, and indeed still is, with his extravagant manner and opinion of himself. But the gambling did for him.

I have also come to the aid of a certain Mrs Davis, a clergyman's widow, by buying her a good house in South Parade, furnished, with a small annuity. She will take lodgers, and I understand that Dean and Mrs Patrick Delaney from Ireland are to visit in at the end of the summer.

Mrs Patrick Delaney was an extraordinarily accomplished figure of the time, and she left an astonishing legacy of botanical and artistic beauty in her *Flora Delanica*, ten volumes of exquisite cut-paper paintings of plants and flowers. She was already well known for her accomplishments and charm when she and her Irish husband lodged with Mrs Davis in Bath in 1760. She observed of Ralph Allen: 'How well does that man deserve the prosperous fortune he has met with'.

DIARY
October 26 1760

The King is dead. His Majesty George the Second died yesterday. I believe things may be very different, for it is known there is little love lost between the new King and William Pitt. Also it will mean the severance of my contract with the Post Office. I would hope that the new contract will swiftly be approved but I suspect there will have to be some negotiation. If Lord Newcastle remains as First Lord of the Treasury, I believe I can count on his support... I shall have to go to London within the month, I fancy.

But the office of Postmaster General was now filled by two new incumbents, the Earl of Bessborough and the Honourable Robert Hampden. Allen sent his petition for the new contract to Lord Newcastle, but it was Bessborough and Hampden who noticed a clause in the contract that no one previously had addressed. Despite Allen's description of how his service had contributed to the "Enlarged and yet Enlarging Correspondence" of the nation, especially with regard to trade, they wanted to know why he had never observed the clause which obliged him to furnish annual accounts of his postal system. Taken aback, Allen pointed out that he had an unblemished record of honest and useful service, and asked that he might be allowed a renewal of his contract without having to undertake a full accounting, particularly for 'the small remainder of a Life, become so precarious by his age and infirmities'. Bessborough and Hampden were sufficiently moved to allow his contract to be renewed, but only if he compiled all the figures within the year.

DIARY
December 15 1760

Once more I am in the Capital, hoping to confirm the signing of the new Contract. It is exceedingly cold, and in St James's Park the lake is frozen, so there are hundreds of skaters and spectators shouting and whooping on the ice. It is not easy walking here, for the cobbles and granite sets in the streets are both slippery with frozen mud and the dung from the cattle they bring through the centre of the City to the abattoirs. And the noise is overwhelming - hooves clattering, iron tyres screeching, hackney carriages crashing, axles squealing, coachmen and carters and children and dogs... I am always aware of how much good Beau Nash has done for Bath, since there the pavements are paved flat and clean and we have none of the filth so visible here.

I am hopeful that all will go well with the signing of the Contract. I have agreed to extend the bye-way and cross-road posts in many parts of the Kingdom, connecting one part of the service with another, especially in the north. I have promised to increase with frequency of the posts on certain routes from three times a week to six. There will be a new nightly bye-letter post thrice weekly from London to York, Durham, Carlisle, Cockermouth, and many northern towns. It will add three thousand pounds to my annual expense, perhaps more. But I know, and they know that I know, that I have the advantage: could they really refuse to sign, and thus put the whole postal system in jeopardy? Nevertheless I suspect they will not let it end here, even if the Contract is signed as they promise. I await news of it: in the meantime I dine with Mr Pitt this evening in St James's Square.

The Contract was duly signed on December 16, 1760. Allen was right that his postal monopoly was under scrutiny, but for now it was safe. Following his dinner with Secretary of State William Pitt, at which no doubt they discussed what great changes were to come about under the new young George III. Allen also gave Pitt a gift of money. Pitt wrote to him, following the dinner:

Letter from William Pitt MP to Ralph Allen
December 15 1760

Sir
The very affecting token of esteem and affection which you put into my hands last night at parting has left Impressions on my heart which I can neither express nor conceal. If the approbation of the good and wise be our wish, how must I feel the sanction of applause and friendship, accompany'd with such an endearing act of kindness from the best of men? ... May the gracious Heaven long continue to lend you to mankind, and particularly to the happiness of him who is unceasingly with the warmest gratitude, respect, and affection, My Dear Sir

Your most faithful Friend & most obliged humble servant,
W. Pitt.

In February, Beau Nash died in penury, cared for by his long-time mistress Juliana Papjoy in a house beside what is now the Theatre Royal.

DIARY
February 19 1761

So poor old Nash is dead. He never did finish his autobiography. The Journal speaks of his being a 'Gentleman in the Course of his Life universally known, and deservedly respected'. Indeed he was. I may not have been a particular friend, but I saw how his Rules had made Bath a civilised City, and whatever his failings – and they were many, snobbery, ignorance and bombast being but three – he had the City at his heart, and loved it more, I think, than any woman.

I recall on one occasion when Mr James Quin, the actor, was upbraiding him for being charged such exorbitant prices by the people of Bath, Mr Nash replied:

'They have acted by you on truly Christian principles, Mr Quin.'

'How so?' says Quin.

'Why,' resumed Nash, 'you were a stranger, and they took you in.'

'Aye,' rejoined Quin, 'but they have fleeced me, instead of clothed me.'

I will say both men enjoyed the exchange; they may have had their faults, but both were of good humour.

When we worked together in establishing the Hospital, he did not ask for reward other than seeing it built and in use for the sick. I think he was glad to go, for he had long been ill, and saw Bath change from the place he knew as a young man. His Rules are less observed: the gambling laws have made the City less frequented by the aristocracy, and there are now more private parties, fewer occasions when people of all kinds may mix together under his once tyrannical eye. We are, perhaps, more sober, more inward looking. Whether it may be good or bad, I cannot tell. His mistress Juliana Papjoy has been with him these past few years and indeed has nursed him devotedly. She is, they say, distraught without him, talks of going to live in a tree or some such nonsense.

Letter from Ralph Allen to Samuel Richardson
April 8 1761

Sir

I have been much moved by your description of the work undertaken at the Magdalen Hospital in London in offering shelter and care to those women who have repented of their profession in prostitution and wish to better themselves for the future. Indeed I would do more than support your own generosity to this institution, and intend to donate ten guineas annually to the Magdalen.

Yours etc.
Ralph Allen

Letter from Ralph Allen to William Pitt MP
October 12 1761

Sir

Mr Yorke, Solicitor General, has been here at Prior Park these past few days and has thus been able to describe the bitter tensions within the King's Government. You know that you have my warmest admiration, despite my own struggle to reconcile certain divisions within my own mind over this question of whether or not to pursue war with Spain. You are implacable that it is in our interests: I am less certain. However I am writing to the Postmasters General to demonstrate that the war has undoubtedly been profitable to the Nation, since the gross produce of postage on bye and cross-road letters has increased some twenty-four per cent since hostilities commenced in 1755 – and indeed, I too have benefited from the rise. But I am also plagued with demands for more Bath stone for St Bartholomew's Hospital, and as you are aware, only Peace would enable me to comply. I do not know which way to be persuaded. Nevertheless whatever the opinions on every side, I cannot but feel sadness for the Nation and sympathy for yourself following your resignation, much as I can see it was inevitable, given the opposition from the King and Lord Bute – indeed, from your fellow MP from Bath, Lord Ligonier, who I believe has argued that the army is not ready for war.

The Journal here today is full of your resignation, printing a list of your victories around the globe, and saying that a few Days will see you reinstated, to the "satisfaction of all true Lovers of the King and Country's interest".

Your faithful friend,
Mr Allen

William Pitt was not reinstated. He accepted an annuity of £3,000 from King George III, and a peerage for his wife, Lady Hester, who became Baroness Chatham – in 1766 Pitt himself went to The House of Lords as Viscount Pitt and Earl of Chatham.

DIARY
November 28 1761

Samuel Prynn has died. It was a sad day. He has been my chief clerk for more than twenty-five years. He has been a faithful friend as well as a man in whom I had complete trust, who was more than capable of all the work I have demanded of him. I feel unconscionably alone without his presence. However I am fortunate that his son Samuel will take his place, and that I have young Philip (Philip Allen, his nephew) to assist me in the task I have now to carry out: that is, the preparation of my accounts for the year to present to the Postmasters General. That is, for the year ending at Midsummer.

The accounts show a gross receipt of about £31,300 in postage, thereby allowing me a net profit of some £12,500. Indeed, I am aware the figures are larger than otherwise, partly because of the successful war and the vast increase of commerce under the protection of it – I do not expect them to continue so high after the approaching establishment of peace.

I have to justify these profits: I am aware of the critical eyes upon them. So I will have to describe the lamentable condition of the postal service before 1720, and my never-ending attempts since then to introduce order, honesty and efficiency. Although the annual rent I have paid has never been increased beyond £6,000, I have agreed in each renewed contract to add more routes, faster deliveries, and more employees all over the country, entirely at my own expense. Therefore I have decided I shall accompany the figures with a 'Narrative', as if a history told by another, so that those addressing the accounts will have an understanding of what lies behind them. My current difficulties with asthma and the gravel make me all too aware of my mortality. Not only do I wish the present contract to be renewed, but I would hope that Philip will inherit the business, for he understands completely how I have managed the postal system, and I know that he will continue my work in the same spirit of dignity and honour.

Ralph Allen's contract for the postal services was renewed that same December, following receipt of his accounts and the 'Narrative' by the Postmasters General and the First Lord of the Treasury, Lord Newcastle.

DIARY
December 29 1761

The year has ended on a better note. Not only has my contract been renewed – indeed I have just sent a letter of gratitude for his goodness to Lord Newcastle – but three days ago, just after Christmas, we had the pleasure of entertaining the young Duke of York (brother of King George III) here at Prior Park. He is of course not the boy we first met that summer three years ago at Weymouth, when he enjoyed open house with his comrades in the fleet, and we offered a little more formality – but he was not much altered in character.

We had a visit from Mr Lancelot Brown in September: he is of course known as 'Capability Brown' because he suggests that the landscape upon which he looks is "capable of improvement", but I never heard him utter such a phrase to me, although he did say he could improve the gardens here at Prior Park. He says they are a little too ornamented, and should be simpler, more in tune with the beauty of this natural valley combe with the view beyond. I find, tho a little reluctant at first, that I agree with him, and so have asked him to put his own mark upon it

The discovery of bills relating to Capability Brown's work at Prior Park shows that he did put his own stamp upon the garden. He was critical of Alexander Pope's cascade and statues, and although he liked the Palladian bridge he thought the landscape too cluttered. The National Trust has now restored much of Pope's original ideas for the garden while retaining Brown's later vision of a natural scene, so that it is possible to see how garden fashion changed from the early to the later eighteenth century.

DIARY
December 20 1762

I have been reflecting on this past year as we approach its end. It has had its good moments, but a certain melancholy pervades: perhaps it is simply that not only the year, but I, approach the end.

Another death earlier this year, that of Samuel Richardson, whose novels I have so much enjoyed, and whose company and friendship I have valued. And more crises in the Government: Lord Newcastle resigned as First Lord of the Treasury on the 24 of May. I wrote to offer my gratitude for all he had done for the nation, and indeed for me, over the years. I cannot but find it ironic that the feeling in the country has shifted back to support for Mr Pitt: in July he made a triumphal visit here to Bath, and we gave a dinner in his honour here at Prior Park. Only a few days ago he made an appearance in the House of Commons, tho' he had to be carried in, so ill has he been, and made a speech of more than three hours attacking the Earl of Bute's terms for the peace. He insisted that the peace would be insecure and inadequate, and that we must have commercial advantage over the French. But Bute was resolute in opposition. It is sad to see Mr Pitt become somewhat arrogant and extreme, for I know it is in great part due to his illness.

In September we also received the Lord Chancellor here to dine with us, for he had come to take the Waters, and we had much talk of the old days when he had been "a-courting" here in Bath. He has an honest way with him that is much to my taste.

October was marked for us by the publication of the 'Life of Richard Nash, Esq'. It was most enjoyable, though of course much of the content was familiar to us, but it is exceedingly well written, by all accounts by a young Irishman called Oliver Goldsmith. I never had the pleasure of meeting him but I am mentioned as "the good Mr Allen" – and that is quite sufficient for me, particularly as in Bath in the same month was Mr Smollett, who would never call me such... He has written a paper called 'The Briton', defending Lord Bute and his opposition to any hostilities with Germany. Seeing as he dedicated his 'Complete History of England' to Mr Pitt, only five years past, it argues quite astounding and probably venal inconsistency – and Mr Smollett has had the audacity to claim that Mr Pitt, not he, has shifted his position.

We have had good company from the family, and I have continued to look after Mr Fielding's widow Sarah and her children. I subscribed to her 'Memoirs of Socrates' this year, with three copies for myself, three for Elizabeth, and one each for my nephew Philip and nieces Gertrude and Molly. Gertrude has not been well and she and Molly did some travelling for "air and exercise" prescribed by her physician. We joined with them to travel to London, leaving Mr Warburton behind at Prior Park – unfortunately he had to share his sojourn with Billy Tucker, who was back from the navy and suffering from a lingering gout... I doubt they had much to talk about.

Letter from Ralph Allen to Mr Biggs, Manager at St Bartholomew's Hospital, London
January 8 1763

Sir

I am much concerned by your news that there has been some deterioration of the stonework on the earlier wings of the Hospital. I had expected some weathering, particularly in view of the polluted atmosphere of London, but it is sad to have to ask you to repair all defects in the stonework. Let me know precisely the condition of the stone.

Yours etc
Mr Allen

On February 10th, 1763, the Treaty of Paris was signed by Great Britain, France, and Spain. It marked the end of a war which had begun in 1756 and encompassed countries all across the globe. It has been estimated that between 900,000 and a million and a half people died in what was thereafter known as The Seven Years War. Churchill was to describe it as the first World War. But it was not received with universal rejoicing – far from it.

In April a journal called *The North Briton*, itself a satirical version of a pamphlet called *The Briton* published by the Prime Minister, the Scottish Earl of Bute, caused a stir. It was written by John Wilkes, a friend of William Pitt's. (John Wilkes was a friend of Thomas Potter, who had talked of seducing Allen's niece Gertrude when she was first married to Bishop Warburton). It contained a vitriolic attack on the Government, in particular the Peace with

France, and there is little doubt that Pitt was complicit, King George III saw it as an attack on the honour of the crown. Wilkes was arrested with 49 others and put in the Tower of London – for a while. He said he was protected by parliamentary privilege, and soon released. He was also the focus of popular support: people saw him as a champion of liberty. Pitt was on his side.

But Ralph Allen could not go along with his respected old friend. There is little doubt that William Pitt had become more aloof, more cruel, in his attitudes, than before. And Allen could not ignore the fact that his latest contract with the Post Office was terminable at the will of the First Lord of the Treasury, now hostile to Pitt. Warburton said the *North Briton* article was a shocking insult to the King: furthermore he had ever regarded war and bloodshed as the 'opprobrium of Christianity'.

In addition, Allen was still worrying about the St Bartholomew's Hospital work, which had so plagued him for years past. The Treaty of Paris meant that the seas were open to commerce – and to the transport of Bath stone. To keep attacking the Treaty, signed months ago, when there was in reality no possibility of changing it, was absurd.

In May Ralph Allen, together with sixteen members of the Bath Council, drafted an address to the King, congratulating him on the peace. The word 'untoward' was applied to the peace, but Allen changed it to 'adequate'. On May 28 copies were sent to the two MPs for Bath, one being William Pitt, to present to the King on behalf of the Bath Council. Allen might have hoped that Pitt would moderate his fierce opposition: but if he did not, his old friend would no longer support him. Pitt did not moderate his views. And the word 'adequate' enraged him, for he saw the Treaty of Paris as giving away much that Britain had vigorously, and with much loss, fought for.

Letter from William Pitt MP to Ralph Allen
June 2 1763

Sir

The epithet of adequate given to the peace contains a description of the conditions of it, so repugnant to my unalterable opinion concerning many of them, and fully declared by me in parliament, that it was as impossible for me to obey the commands of the corporation in presenting their address, as it as unexpected to receive such a commission.

As to my opinion of the peace, I will only say, that I formed it with sincerity, according to such lights as my little experience and small portion of understanding could afford me. This conviction must remain to myself the constant rule of my conduct; and I leave to others, with much deference to their better information, to follow their own judgment...

With respectful and affectionate esteem, and my compliments to all at Prior Park,

Your faithful friend,
William Pitt.

Allen replied to this bitter irony:

Letter from Ralph Allen to William Pitt MP
June 4 1763

Sir

It is extremely painful to me to find... that the word <u>adequate</u> in the Bath address has been so very offensive to you, as to hinder the sincerest and most zealous of your friends in the corporation from testifying for the future their great attachment to you.

Upon this occasion, in justice to them, it is incumbent on me to acquaint you, that the exceptionable word does not rest with them, but myself; who suddenly drew up that address to prevent their sending off another, which the mayor brought to me, in terms that I could not concur in... I shall decline executing your commands to the corporation on this delicate point; unless you renew them upon your perusal of this letter, which, for safety, I have sent by a messenger; and I beg your answer to it by him, who has orders to wait for it.

Permit me to say, that I have not the least objection to, but feel the highest regard and even veneration for, your whole conduct; neither have I any apology to make for the expression in which I am so unfortunate as to differ from you. And with the utmost respect, affection, and gratitude, you will always find me to be, my dearest Sir,

Your most humble and most obedient servant
R. Allen

Pitt did send his reply by the waiting messenger, but still regretted that his ideas differed widely from 'those of the man whose goodness of heart and private virtues I shall ever respect and love'. He asked Allen to deliver his earlier letter to the Mayor and Council, confirming his refusal to present the congratulatory address to King George.

Letter from William Pitt MP to Ralph Allen
June 4 1763

Sir

    …I am not insensible to your kind motives for wishing to interpose time for second thoughts; but, knowing how much you approve an open and ingenuous proceeding, I trust that you will see the unfitness of my concealing from my constituents the insurmountable reasons which prevented my obeying your commands, in presenting an address containing a disavowal of my opinion delivered in Parliament relating to the peace. As their servant, I owe to these gentlemen an explanation of my conduct on this occasion; and a man not forgetful of the distinguished honour of having been invited to represent them, I owe it in gratitude to them not to think of embarrassing and encumbering for the future, friends to whom I have such obligations, and who now view with approbation measures of an administration, founded on the subversion of that system which once procured me the countenance and favour of the city of Bath.

Your humble friend and servant,
W. Pitt

Allen did as Pitt has asked, and delivered the letter. There is no formal record of what took place in the Bath Council, but Allen wrote again to Pitt, justifying what some might have said was a betrayal.

Letter from Ralph Allen to William Pitt MP
June 8 1763

Sir

Upon this disagreeable occasion give me leave just to say, that however different our abilities may be, it is the duty of every honest man, after he has made the strictest inquiry, to act pursuant to the light which the Supreme Being has been pleased to dispense to him; and this being the rule that I am persuaded we both govern ourselves by, I shall take the liberty now only to add, that it is impossible for any person to retain higher sentiments of your late glorious administration than I do, nor can be with truer fidelity, zeal, affection and respect than I have been, still am, and always shall be, my dearest Sir,

Your most humble and most obedient servant
R. Allen

But the difference between them became public. Allen was seen to have acted in a high handed and autocratic manner in making the Bath Council send the offending address. Cartoons appeared, championing Pitt and satirising not only the Earl of Bute as a devil in a Scottish tartan, but Bishop Warburton (thought to have influenced Allen) and Ralph Allen himself. The first, called 'The Knights of Baythe, or the One-headed Corporation', depicted the Council as a faceless group of men beside a large, clear portrait of Allen himself, with a Cornish chough perched on top of his wig, croaking "Raafe, Raafe, poor Raafe". The second – 'A Sequel' – repeats the accusation that Allen had betrayed Pitt, and this time on top of the Cornish chough is a postboy on his horse, blowing his horn. It was, perhaps, a reference to the fact that the renewal of Allen's postal service contract was at the mercy of a Treasury hostile to Pitt.

DIARY
December 19 1763

Young Philip Allen, my dear nephew, was married
two days ago at St James's Church, Westminster,
to Sarah Carteret. The Journal today describes
her as "a beautiful Lady with £10,000 fortune".
Well, so she is. Both her parents are dead and her
father was of an ancient and wealthy family. Yet
what the Journal – thankfully – does not know is
that I have also arranged for my brother Philip
to receive £6,000 in bank annuities so that Philip
might give this money to his son for settlement on
the bride at marriage, half to be held in trust for
her. It will not be publicly known until my Will is
read after my death.

My eyes are causing me great trouble. I wonder
if the difficulties of this year have been in part to
blame. We escaped to Weymouth in the summer
and thereby had some respite from the public
opprobrium, but there was still much unpleasantness
abroad in the City when we returned to Bath. I
know that there was discussion in the Council of
my being elected Mayor again, although in the end
they passed a motion excusing me from serving
in that office. I felt obliged then to send a formal
letter to the Major and Council begging them to
allow me to resign as Alderman, on account of my
failing eyesight and general health. I promised
loyalty to the City, of course, and could not help
but remind the Council of my promised gift of £500
towards a new Town Hall. Yet although at the
next meeting a motion was offered to thank me for

my many services, the vote was not unanimous. I know from my nephews, Philip and Ralph, that Mr George Scott is probably responsible for continuing the hostility. Indeed, he has apparently called me a 'mushroom', and described me as having Pride, Insolence and Vanity...

Mr William Strahan, a London printer who has recently been taking the waters, dined here at Prior Park some little while ago, and most kindly suggested that he might secure a reading glass for me in London. He was true to his word, and being much taken with little Ralph Warburton [then five years old, the son of Gertrude and Warburton, now Bishop of Gloucester] he not only sent me the glass, but a variety of books "to allure him to read a little more than he might otherwise incline". We have had much pleasure, the boy and I, of therefore reading some old favourites together.

But what has given me particular comfort has been some lessening of the estrangement between myself and Mr Pitt. He has sold his house in the Circus, but remains MP, and his desperately failing health obliges him to spend considerable time here having treatment for his ailments. Indeed, I have added a codicil to my will: "For the last instance of my friendship and grateful regard for the best of friends, as well as the most upright and ablest of Ministers that has adorned our country, I give to the Right Honourable William Pitt the sum of £1,000, to be disposed of by him to any one of his children that he may be pleased to appoint for it".

The Circus had recently been completed by John Wood the Younger. Pitt had been one of the first to buy one of the leasehold houses, No. 7.

DIARY
March 19 1764

I suppose it is because he was a Cornishman himself, as well as a true old friend, that I feel so cast down by the news of the death of Dr Oliver. He was loved by all, I do believe. He was always interested in everything about him, he made one feel better through the simple power of his character, let alone his skill as a physician. It is a great loss and I feel it more than I can say.

DIARY
May 22 1764

More troubles with St Bartholomew's Hospital. It has seemed as if all my life I have had to contend with what at first seemed so promising a project. Richard Biggs himself is old, now. He is still there, supervising the masons, but there seem to be ever higher bills for labour, for the sea freight of the stone, for the unloading, and, since it has been unseasonably hot, for beer... The work is not going well. There are breaks and crumblings in the older sections of the stone. It is, I fancy, like me, ageing, and perhaps in need of repair. For the stone it can be done. For me, I think I am beyond repair.

Soon afterwards Allen set out on a coach journey to London, but became so ill that he had to turn back. His old Clerk of Works, Richard Jones, wrote in his later account of this time:

> "When Mr Allen found his death approaching, he went with me, and chose out the spot of ground where his vault and monument should be in the churchyard…about five days before he died he sent for me to bring him the drawings of the burial place, and told me if he lived any time he would see it done in his lifetime, and ordered me to leave it till the next day, which I did, and before I saw him again, he died."

On the morning of June 27 Allen expressed his desire to be buried as privately and decently as possible, without pomp, in the churchyard at Claverton, and pointed out that the drawings for the tomb and an inscription for it were in the second drawer of the chest nearest his bed. The next day he signed a new copy of his will and codicils, confirming that bequeathing £1,000 to William Pitt, whom with his last breath he wished to honour. He died on the morning of June 29, 1764. He was 71.

EPILOGUE

Ralph Allen was buried on July 5 in the little church in Claverton.

His tomb was in due course built in Claverton churchyard. It remains, although the old house he loved there was demolished, though replaced by a fine manor.

Mrs Elizabeth Allen inherited Prior Park, the house in Weymouth and an annuity for her lifetime, but she lived for only two years after her husband's death, and Gertrude, wife of Bishop Warburton, then inherited it together with the main part of his estate.

He left many bequests, chiefly to members of his family. He also left money to some employees and servants such as the young Samuel Prynn, and his body-servant Breedon. Richard Jones received £45, a year's wage but perhaps not as much as he might have expected. However in his rather fanciful autobiography he accuses Warburton and Gertrude of meanness, not Allen. The executors of the estate struggled to find the cash to pay Allen's bequests and had to sell sheep, saddle horses and many other items, as well as shares and securities. The contract with St Bartholomew's Hospital was still extant and was not completed until two years after Allen's death.

Gertrude was 38 years old when she inherited Prior Park, and enjoyed being its mistress for a while: Charles Yorke called her 'my honoured Landlady of the Enchanted

Castle'. Figures such as David Garrick and Gainsborough still visited. But without the income from the Post Office it was difficult to maintain. In 1769, five years after Allen's death, Gertrude decided that she and Warburton should vacate the mansion, sell off the contents and lease it. A grand auction was held in August. The catalogue ran to 28 pages, including such items as pictures, 320 sheep and lambs, maps, library steps, a cradle and coal.

The young Ralph Warburton, the child of Bishop Warburton's old age – and still by some rumoured to be the natural son of the rake Thomas Potter – had been a favourite of Ralph Allen. The old man and the little boy had been friends. But in 1775, at the age of only 19, he died of some rapid 'consumption'. Bishop Warburton never recovered from the blow and died four years later. He left a legacy of his and Allen's library to Richard Hurd, Allen's quiet friend who remained as an advisor to Gertrude. Hurd became Bishop of Worcester, and in 1780 he housed the books in a fine room specially built at his palace in Worcestershire, Hartlebury Castle. Above the shelves of this long library gallery he placed portraits of Alexander Pope, William Warburton and Ralph Allen.

Gertrude cared for her husband until he died. In her early fifties she married again. Her second husband was her first husband's chaplain and was some twenty years younger than she was. She died in 1796, aged 68.

The Government took over Ralph Allen's postal empire in the September of 1764, but appointed Philip Allen as Comptroller of the Bye and Cross-Road Letter Office – at a much reduced salary. He and his descendants preserved the Allen name at Bathampton Manor for another 150 years.

When he was told of the death of Allen, William Pitt wrote to Mrs Allen:

> "…in Mr Allen, mankind has lost such a benevolent and tender friend as, I fear, not all the example of his virtues will have power to raise up to the world his like again. Admiring his life, and deploring the shortness of it, I shall ever respectfully cherish his memory, and rank the continuation of the favourable opinion and friendship of a truly good man amongst the happiest advantages and the first honours, which fortune may have bestowed upon my life".

SOURCES

Addison, Peter. *Around Combe Down,* Millstream Books (1998)

Anstey, Christopher. *The New Bath Guide.* First published 1766

Bezzant, Norman. *Out of the Rock,* William Heinemann (1981)

Boyce, Benjamin. *The Benevolent Man: A Life of Ralph Allen of Bath,* Cambridge: Harvard University Press (1967)

Cunliffe, Barry. *Roman Bath Discovered,* Routledge & Kegan Paul 1971

Fawcett, Trevor. *Georgian Imprints,* Ruton (2008)

Fielding, Henry. *The Life and Death of Jonathan Wild.* First published 1743

Fielding, Henry. *The History of Tom Jones, a Foundling.* First published 1749

Fiennes, Celia. *Illustrated Journeys* edited by Christopher Morris Macdonald (1982)

Forsyth, Michael. *Bath – Pevsner Architectural Guide.* Yale University Press (2007)

Hill, Mary K. *Bath and the 18th Century Novel,* Bath University Press (1989)

Kilvert, Francis. *Kilvert's Diary.* First published 1938-40

Peach, R. E. M. *Bath, Old and New.* First published 1888

Picard, Liza. *Dr Johnson's London,* Phoenix Press (2001)

Plumb, J. H. *England in the Eighteenth Century,* Penguin (1950)

Scott, Maurice. *Discovering Widcombe and Lyncombe, Bath,* The Widcombe Association (1993)

Smollett, Tobias. *The Expedition of Humphrey Clinker.* First published 1771

Winsor, Diana. *The Dream of Bath,* Trade & Travel Publications (1981)

Woodward, Christopher. *The Building of Bath,* The Building of Bath Museum.

The author gratefully acknowledges the assistance of the Building of Bath Collection, the British Library, the Victoria and Albert Museum, Dan Brown of Bath in Time, Bath Central Library and many others.

THE AUTHOR

Diana Winsor has been a journalist since the 1960s, writing for several newspapers and magazines, including the *Sunday Times* and the *Daily Telegraph*, both as a staff writer and a freelance. She is the author of two thrillers, *Red on Wight* and *The Death Convention* (Macmillan, 1972 and 1974). In 1980 she wrote *The Dream of Bath*, and in 1983 *Britain - A Country Compass*. Her most recent book is *Mr Brouard's Odyssey*, published in 2004. She has also written many short stories and contributed to several books on Britain, among them *Yesterday's Britain* and *Discovering Britain* for Reader's Digest Books. She is married with two daughters and lives in Worcestershire, although a frequent visitor to Bath where her mother still lives, close to one of Ralph Allen's stone quarries. She also paints and is working for her first exhibition in 2011.